THE EMPOWERED AFFIRMATIONS TECHNIQUE

By

Veronica Lavender

Published   3/10/2014

ISBN-13: 978-1497532861

ISBN-10: 1497532868

Other Books by Author

The Essential Creativity of Awareness

Parallel Lives

Embrace the Power Within

Jack the Ripper & the Ghost of Mary Jane Kelly

DISCLAIMER

I have put The Empowered Affirmations Technique book together has a guideline for an aid for Well Being; it is therefore your own personal choice to take part in any of the techniques described has a possible way of increasing self-knowledge and understanding, and the releasing of negative blocks or disharmonious situations within the energy system by using this technique. I therefore taken no responsibility and no legal actions can be taken against me.

ACKNOWLEDGEMENTS

I would like to say thank you to my children, Debbie, David and Karen who have given me love and support, whilst pursuing my dreams. They continue to be a great inspiration to me with their encouragement. To my dear friends who have given me hours of discussions and debates, on all aspects of spirituality.

I would like to thank all readers of my other books, and also to all that have touched my life in so many different ways. You have all inspired me which has allowed me to gain a greater understanding of how the mind, body and soul works together, influencing all that we do. Thank you.

INTRODUCTION

The Empowered Affirmations Technique is designed to help those who want to understand and overcome why they feel blocked within their lives. Our life's pathways are pre-destined, and what happens to us is part of our life's purpose and lessons that we must experience, all being part of the divine plan. We are all living this lifetime with the sole intention of us claiming back our true identities, our unique gifts, skills, and abilities which reconnect us to our infinite power within. This process will reconnect us to our limitless potential of all lifetimes, and the blueprint of our souls.

When we reconnect with our unique power within, allows us to re-establish our connection with the infinite power of the universe, and our creator. This connection allows us to heal our lives consciously and on all levels of existence. When we heal the mind, body, and soul, we connect to our higher conscious self, and that of our personal truth and blueprint of our soul. The secret to living our lives successfully is to achieve balance and harmony by eradicating discomfort, ailments, illness or disease from within our lives. This process allows us to feel content and fulfilled, within the different aspects of our everyday lives, enabling us to achieve success in all that we do.

The affirmations technique is easy and effective, with us feeling more positive straight away, uplifted and empowered. Once we have a clear vision of what we want to achieve or accomplish within our lives, we can then make choices or confident decisions about our future. This new found awareness allows us to be in control of our everyday lives, and with realistic focus, determination and conviction, allows us to succeed in achieving our goals or dreams.

When we have focused intention we can rebalance our energy field within and around the physical body, which then has a positive effect on the mind that influences, and empowers every aspect of our lives. We then start to attract all that we need in a positive and successful way, allowing us to take back the control of our true destiny and life. We then become consciously aware of our higher conscious self and limitless potential.

The infinite power within is located at the heart, and by simply placing our hand or projecting our minds energy to our heart centre connects us to the collective consciousness of us. This connection allows us to focus on expanding the minds energy which connects us to the infinite energy of our creator. With the reconnection to this unique energy, and the combination of the hearts energy will naturally reignite our infinite power within.

When we recite empowered affirmations with our hand over our heart, it will naturally connect us to our higher conscious-self in order to empower us. The affirmations technique, will allow the negativity from within to be released, with us becoming more positive straight away, and the decisions we then make are on a higher conscious level.

The affirmations technique works with our higher consciousness, whilst connected to our infinite power within the heart centre. By connecting with heart centre, helps us focus on the reprogramming or promises that we are making to our higher conscious self, whilst accessing our truth. This process will allow us to stay focused whilst a shift in our consciousness takes place, and then the command or affirmation allows us to empower ourselves completely allowing our energy field to rebalance. With practice you'll realise that you do not need to place your hand over the heart centre in order to empower the self. It's about connecting with the minds infinite energy as it expands, connecting us at a higher conscious state to the collective consciousness of us, where the thought, command or deed becomes a reality.

The power of affirmations has a profound effect on the mind, body and soul. These affirmations allow us to reprogram old thought patterns and beliefs, altering our perceptions about the different situations or circumstances within our lives. This process has an adverse effect on how the mind then influences the physical body which alters our states of consciousness, and reconnects us to the blueprint of our souls. When we recite positive affirmations, and connect to the infinite life-force energy within our physical bodies and minds, we are able to re-educate us to becoming more self and body-aware. The affirmations that you choose to recite, will give you a deeper understanding of how to achieve success within all areas of your life, and how to create abundance in all that you do.

Once we understand what our negative emotional issues are all about, allows us to recognise what is really happening within our lives. This enables us to choose an appropriate empowered affirmation that will help us to release the negativity that has caused the imbalance or disharmony within. We all have at some time or other found ourselves making the same mistakes over and over again, wondering if we would ever learn or even to comprehend the real reasons behind our current situation or circumstance.

The lack of understanding to what's happening to us can often leave us feeling angry, tried, frustrated, disappointed or resentful, all because the outcome we desired, did not turn out as we had hoped for! We then procrastinate because our efforts of trying to understand or sorting our problems out, was just not good enough. When this happens we take the risk of becoming disheartened which has a negative effect on us. We then find ourselves giving up on our dreams or ambitions when the rewards or goal, are just in sight.

When we stop believing in us, we then doubt us and our unique abilities, all because of the negative imbalances within that we'd not fully understood or even recognised was there. All problems within our lives need to be understood, and then we can solve and release them. We need to reinstate well being before we can successfully accomplish our dreams or ambitions.

We need to eradicate our imbalances or problems, by resolving them, which then set us free from any unwanted influences or distractions. It's important that we try to understand and then remove the obstructions or restrictions from within our lives, and with perseverance and foresight we can consciously change our lives for the better. Through right action, our decisions become clear which allows us to go through our ascension process, easily and effortlessly.

This unique technique can leave you feeling empowered by your own infinite energy, and with the realignment of the mind, body and soul, promotes a well being state. The more evolved we are, the less our physical bodies are effected by our negative emotions, and also that of others. This new understanding alters our mindset and perception, and allows us continued balance and harmony within our everyday lives. This will aid us in achieving our dreams successfully, whilst maintaining a well being and blissful state.

This lifetime is about us all having a heavenly life in a human form, and not the one we've created for us out of unhappiness, and strife. Our higher consciousness is the carbon footprint of all that we've ever been, and to whom we are still to become.

CONTENTS

BALANCE YOUR LIFE

We are now living in The Age of Aquarius where each and every-one of us can achieve our limitless potential. First, we must release our limiting beliefs, negative programs, and the negativity or imbalances that's held within that effects our every-day lives. We are all required and have a responsibility to us, too go through the purification and cleansing process of our sub-conscious and conscious minds, in preparation of eradicating the world's mass-negativity as well as our own.

We are going through this process in order to become more positive and healthier, whilst pursing our dreams or ambitions. This allows us to no longer be influenced by the negativity within our lives that at times we have no control over but has a huge impact on us. It's important that we become our higher conscious self once more which will allows us to transform our lives consciously, whilst accessing our truth of all things but on a higher conscious level.

Each individual is being exposed to their own negative imbalances or blocks so they can overcome and release them. We are also being made aware of the different areas within our lives where we need to make changes, and take positive action into achieving a well being state once more. This can be a daunting task! How do we achieve well being when life's stress and tension has already begun to take its toll on the mind, body or soul, and controls our lives in so many different ways?

What is this new cyclic age all about, and what do we need to do in order to take back the control of our true destiny, and every-day lives whilst achieving all we desire? The Age of Aquarius is about the transformation from our lower conscious self, to the higher conscious self which then aids us on our soul's quest of ascension. Spiritual pathways all have one purpose, for they are not just a way of life but the different methods of achieving a life consciously. We do not find ourselves within the many different cultures or techniques but through them, allowing ourselves the opportunity for continued spiritual and personal growth.

Over the years and the many centuries, our souls have become weary time travellers. This has caused the mind and body to become detached from our truth, and that of the soul's true purpose. With detachment from our personal truth, leaves us struggling to access the higher conscious self which would've helped us to activate, and find the solutions to our problems easily and effortlessly. Instead we are left wondering around in a mental fog, trying to understand what our lives are all about.

The process of being detached from our truth causes us pain and grief, and leaves us not being able to solve the many problems that we can have within our lives. We often find us continuing to make the same mistakes over and over again, whilst trying to sustain a happy and healthy existence. The continuing battles leave us feeling unfulfilled or bored with our chosen vocations or relationships.

Throughout our lifetime, we'll find ourselves travelling many different pathways seeking the opportunities as they present themselves to us, whilst trying to maintain equilibrium between the different aspects of our lives. This process can at times, leaves us feeling unfulfilled or frustrated because we can't bring our dreams or desires into fruition. We need to be in control of us, and not the different aspects of our lives, as this causes us to look in an outwardly direction for the next quick fix, maybe craving rest-bite from our hectic lives.

Holidays make us feel better with us getting away from our everyday lives, but when we get back our problems are still there. The positive side to a holiday is that it takes us away from our current situation, where we stand more of a chance of realising a solution to our problems. Holiday's are great but not always the answer, we need to change the way

2

we perceive what's happening in our lives, because by not recognising the imbalances within, it could leave us craving for some rest-bite, career or relationship change, and so on that could cost us dearly.

Once we understand what's happening to us, we need to reprogram us, and re-ignite the energy within that releases us from the restraints and restrictions that we hold the mind and body too. When we clear the different imbalances from within our lives or us, would re-establish balance between every aspect of us, this allows us to make confident decisions about what we want to do in order to accomplish our dreams successfully.

The affirmations technique works on a higher conscious level, and allows us to realise the truth about any given situation or circumstance that we have experienced or find ourselves in. Once we've understood what's expected from us, we can then overcome our problems, with us being able to release any negativity that's associated with them, and that's held within our mind, body or soul. When we have located our negative beliefs, thoughts or programs, we can set about releasing them consciously, empowering us to achieve the very best from life. We then use our natural gifts, skills and abilities, to their limitless potential.

When we empower the mind and body with positive affirmations or thoughts, empowers the soul which reconnects us with our truth of all situations. When we become our higher conscious self, we can access the Akasha records and the esoteric knowledge of all that we've ever been or accomplished, since time began. This is called our infinite knowledge and wisdom, and allows us to have a positive mindset once more, with us taking back the controls of our true destiny and lives. We then attain the life that was intended for us, instead of the one that we've created from our insecurities or unhappiness.

So with the help of this technique we're able to release the negativity from within by reconnecting to our own infinitive power. We connect with this by placing our hand over the heart which naturally connects us to our true-selves, and higher consciousness. It also allows us to be at one with us where a profound healing takes place, altering our perception and understanding of our insecurities. When we recite an empowered affirmation it will help to rebalance our energy within and around our physical body. This aids us in achieving the ultimate connection to our higher consciousness which allows a healing of the mind, body, and soul to take place. This gives us a firm connection to the source of the universal energy of our creator and higher conscious us, whilst we achieve all that we desire.

The healing process allows us to become empowered by our new thoughts, and a powerful re-programming which allows us to take positive action in achieving our dreams, goals or ambitions, whilst accessing our unique gifts, skills and abilities of our intuitiveness and knowing thoughts. These are our natural gifts that help us to overcome all obstacles whilst in pursuit of achieving a great life for us, and our families.

We all at sometime or other disconnected from our truth, gifts, skills and abilities all because of the illusions within our lives, which left us trying to cope the best way we could. With us taking the risk of allowing our immunity to close down, and no longer being able to ward off infections or illness. This causes us to experience ill health or disease, all because we didn't believe, have faith or trust in us anymore, and in the process of our life unfolding naturally.

In order to maintain well being we need to re-simulate, and re-energise the immune centre which is closely connected to the heart centre. The combination of the two has a powerful effect on the body's own inner life-force energy and healing abilities. There is a constant supply of infinite universal energy that flows freely throughout our entire physical and mental system, feeding all of the organs, muscles, skeleton, cells, in-fact the whole of our bodies, including the meridians and acupuncture points within.

The stimulus of all of these intricate organs exacta is important in us achieving a healthy existence within our lives once more. With balance and harmony restored to the mind, body and soul, gives us realignment to the earth, universe and cosmic energies, which reinstates our birthright, and our place to be in unity, and within all aspects of our unique world. We can then successfully achieve balance and harmony with all things, and reinstate the connection to the creator and the collective consciousness of our unique world.

I am a Theta Healer Practitioner working with the universal energy of the creator to achieve a Well Being state whilst unleashing my limitless potential. The connection with this infinite energy enables us all to self heal, and with simple commands, affirmations or positive thoughts, will allow us to release any imbalance, illness or disease that's harboured within us, once we've acknowledged and accepted the truth of any given situation or condition. This process is life changing, and can be done easily and effortlessly, with a commitment to ourselves to restore health, happiness, and well being to our mind, body and soul, once more.

During the Theta Healing training, the tutor recited to us affirmations to empower us. These affirmations were called the creators downloads, they were the creators definition of how he wanted us to perceive our true feelings in order to re-educate us into understanding what true happiness, joy, love, compassion and so on, really felt like. Up till receiving the creator's definition of happiness excreta, I'd only my perception of what true happiness felt like. My perception of happiness was tainted by my life's experiences, and too what had happened to me.

If we're not happy it's because we've stopped us from being so, all because of our perception of what had happened to us. When I received the creator's version of happiness, it was hypothetically my higher consciousness' definition as opposed to my lower conscious perception. The whole process was very empowering because I realized that I'd stopped myself from being really happy, all because I hadn't recognised what was really important to me, and what I did have within my life, as opposed to what I didn't.

At times we all lose sight of what's important, maybe not recognising what we already have within our lives, until it's too late. If we can change the way we perceive things, and by accepting our truth of any given situation, will allow us to let go of our limiting beliefs or fears in order to succeed. To be truly happy with every aspect of our lives needs recognition of how lucky we really are, and to how much we've already accomplished or overcome. This gives us faith, belief and trust in us, which promotes self love, worth and self-esteem.

When receiving positive affirmations or downloads they show us that we can live our every-day lives without fear or a lack of confidence, faith, trust or belief in us. We empower ourselves to know how to, and more importantly when too change the things within our lives that no longer serve our higher conscious us. We can empower us with the different aspect of understanding the real us, and our feelings in their truest form, such as success, confidence, health, commitment, in fact any perceived emotion, feeling or belief.

Until we empower us with affirmations, all we have is our perception of these emotions, feelings or beliefs before we're enlightened, and our perception of our emotions, feelings or beliefs afterwards, are commonly known as our truth. Our feelings or beliefs are unjustifiable when in their truest form. In other words, our truest form and the understanding of happiness excreta, is about our level of consciousness at the time. Our conscious awareness grows with personal and spiritual growth of understanding, and overcoming all limitations of our negative feelings, beliefs, and programs.

Our Creator wants us all to have the life that was intended, instead of the one we've created for us, all because of our disconnection from the truth. This truth is the collective truth of mankind and all of creation, but most of all that of our own personal truth when reinstated would allow us to become a powerful being once more. The majority of us have become disconnected from our truth during this lifetime or even over many centuries. This lifetime is about the reconnection of our truth that's stored within our higher conscious self which is the blueprint of our soul.

We can only reconnect with our truth once we've understood and overcome our life's purpose. The way we then perceive our life's experiences from that moment on, would have a huge impact on us, and the overall outcome of our decisions or choices would be very positive. By understanding what we've done to us and by letting it go, we can reinstate well being, with us being instantly connected to our truth of any given situation or circumstance. This would make us accepting of all situations, with us becoming successful in all that we do. We no longer feel threatened, a victim or feel we're being punished in some-way. Our lives become joyous, with us having a positive and optimistic outlook in life.

These affirmations will help to reform and refocus us, on what's really important within our lives. The new thought pattern or program, will help us to understand the different aspects of lives that we'd once struggled with, giving us a deeper understanding of our life's purpose and lessons which allows us to achieve our limitless potential of all lifetimes.

During my Theta healing training we were all asked to stand upright, whilst we accepted downloads of the creator's affirmation or definition of happiness, contentment, love, joy and so on. We stood with our feet apart for balance, and as the commands for each download was given, I swayed back and forth. The process was very empowering, and the experience of how some of the affirmations made me sway gently, and others made me sway quite dramatically, was mind blowing. I realised that some of the affirmations or understanding of those affirmations was already within, and I just needed to rebalance to them once more. Where the other downloads that had made me sway quite dramatically, and only after further examination, I understood to be that my emotional feelings, insecurities, negative beliefs or traits, were still held within, because I hadn't dealt with or understood them properly, but they were still influencing me negatively.

With further understanding of my feelings, and the process work to unearth my deep rooted issues, allowed my negative emotions or imbalances to come to the surface in order for me to deal with them properly. I was then able to release the imbalance from within to allow the download or affirmation to take a positive effect, and empower me completely. This gave me a positive outlook in which to pursue my goals and desires, with a clear vision of what I wanted to accomplish, and of the outcome.

What I've understood from the various holistic techniques that I've used over the years, is our perception is not always about our truth but about self preservation of survival. When we analyze the different negative aspect of us, allows us to set us free from the restraints and restrictions that we hold us too. I believe we need to empower us with our higher consciousness' definition of the different aspects of health, happiness, joy, compassion and so on. Our lower conscious us has us struggling, where our higher consciousness is the crusader of truth, and with rightful action will influence us through the mire of our negative beliefs or illusions in order for us to succeed by accomplishing our dreams or goals.

We can empower us to achieve things beyond our wildest dreams, because we're all unique to us and our levels of truth, and the definition of what we perceive differs and alters with our ability to adjust to the different levels of initiation and the transformation of our spiritual reawakening and personal growth.

There are lots of different methods or techniques that are readily available to us in order to experience and achieve a well being state. So allow yourself to be drawn to what's right for you, and start the process of a self-discovery journey which will allow us all to heal every aspect of our lives eventually.

The new age of Aquarius will allow all of us to activate our own personal gifts, skills, and abilities that will allow us to naturally realize and release the imbalances from within. We must fully understand the importance of these unique gifts, with us aiming to become a highly evolved human being, in order to achieve a successful life in the present time, whilst inspiring and helping others to do likewise.

The empowered affirmations that I have designed are more encompassing, and will aid us in connecting with our higher conscious self, and true self once more. This process will allow us to empower ourselves at any time, taking back the control of our everyday lives.

We can empower us to achieve success in all that we desire or pursue with conviction and courage. Maybe you've applied for your dream job, and you're fearful about the interview process, suffering from a lack of self-confidence, belief or faith that the job could be truly yours. By empowering yourself, you can manifest a successful outcome by already seeing yourself doing the job, which then gives you more commitment and focus, in achieving and securing the job. You must be confident that you want the job for the right reasons, because it's not always about an increase in salary, it's about you accomplishing your true vocation or mission in life.

When we connect to our infinite energy within, it will allow us to be fully in our lives once more, and aids us in feeling contentment and fulfilment, in all that we do. It also encourages us to help not just ourselves but others to understand their life's purpose, allowing us all to become our limitless potential of all lifetimes. It is important that we're fully in our lives, with us happily communicating with others, because we're all connected. When connected to the family of life, is important to our continued growth, where we all learn and help each other to evolve.

Our Life's journey is to reconnect with our personal truth, accessed at a higher conscious level. This is our life's mission, fulfilling the promise that we all made to us long ago, and before we were born into this lifetime. This is the promise to reconnect with the ultimate power of divinity that's within, and is the unique power of us and our creator, the definitive power that sustains all life. This is our personal power! So when experiencing the technique, and after you have recited your chosen affirmation, you say! I am my infinite power because that is our truth. Regardless of what's happened to us within this life, it's about our level of conscious awareness at the time.

The process of self healing is to be self-aware, body-aware, emotionally-aware and spiritually-aware, in order for us to heal every aspect of our lives, but more importantly to be consciously-aware of what we are doing, saying, thinking or manifesting. Life is a great adventure, and it's important that we all live our lives to the full whilst achieving our dreams or goals.

It's important that we don't bury our heads in the sand, hoping that our problems will go away, because they don't. The deeper rooted problems will manifest themselves over and over again with us becoming disheartened or discouraged until we do sort them out. With commitment, faith, belief and trust, we can overcome all our problems when it's right for us to do so. Until then, in accepting what's happened or happening will allow us to stay positive, in order to override the storm or challenges, with us eventually succeeding in all we do. We then learn our lessons or purpose through the process of understanding and overcoming our life's experiences, good or bad.

Occasionally we need to stand back from life, just to see the bigger picture, and to see that others are also struggling with certain aspect of their lives. We could all do with a helping hand or a little encouragement, especially if we hadn't realised the fact that we're struggling in some-way. Other people's kindness can sometimes reduce us to tears, all because we hadn't recognised our feelings or emotions of the unrest within.

We need to be totally honest with us about what we're really feeling within, because we say were alright when in fact were not. By communicating with each other we can then accept the help that we need in order to gain the understanding. This enables us to overcome our life's purpose or lessons by being aware of our needs as well as others, has we all need help from time to time in order to achieve our souls quest.

When we realise that we're not alone in our suffering or hardships, and that every-one of us struggles with the different aspect within our lives, at sometime or other. We all handle or perceive our problems differently, but a problem shared is a problem halved, and then we stand more chance of achieving a solution to any endeavour. We do not have to be on a spiritual journey in order to overcome our problems or issues in life, we just need to recognise that we have a problem, because then we stand more chance of overcoming them by being consciously aware to all situations or circumstances that we may find ourselves in, and is effecting us and our lives greatly.

The unrest within, is our soul reminding us of the promise we made to us long ago of the reconnection to the infinite energy of our higher conscious self. This automatically strengthens are connection to the creators universal energy and collective energy of us. The reconnection of this infinite energy is our true destiny which will make us all powerful human being once more, whilst in pursuit of our intended life of wealth, health and happiness.

SELF AWARENESS

The journey of self awareness is a life changing experience, as each and every-one of us can at times neglect the self, whilst in pursuit of our dreams or ambitions. We often focus on others, because we don't always recognise the need to focus on us, maybe with us thinking that we're ok, when in fact we're not. Self awareness is the journey of self discovery of our truest-self, and the truth of our intended existence whilst we experience, and understand our life purpose. We all need to achieve a higher conscious level in order to overcome our lessons successfully.

I have designed this book to help all who want to understand or take part in their spiritual transformation, to reconnect with their true-self, and understand their bodies many needs. It's important that we become more self aware in order to take back the controls of our true destiny, with us receiving or accomplishing all that we desire, but consciously. Our life's journey is to overcome our lessons by understanding the significance of life's experiences, good or bad. When we accept what's happened to us, and that it was part of our life's learning's, will allow us to overcome them whilst maintaining balance and harmony within every aspect of our lives.

When using this technique, we empower the self with empowered affirmations which reawakens us to our higher conscious self. This leaves us feeling good about every aspect of our lives or self, and makes us consciously aware of a unique power within us. When we listen to our higher conscious self, we're made aware of the disharmonious situations within our lives, mind or body. More importantly, when we listen to that small voice within, it's our intuitiveness guiding or inspiring us, maybe of situations that need attention! We all at sometime or other, hear that small voice within, maybe acting instinctively to what it's said or naturally just going with the flow of inspiration or guidance. On other occasions we totally ignore that small voice, and go ahead regardless of what happens to us, taking the risk of making a wrong decision, which causes pain or grief to us or even others.

Our intuitive self speaks to us all the time, it's that niggling doubt that we still choose to ignore or maybe it's the incredible vision, inspiration or knowing that can often have us achieving things beyond our wildest dreams. By ignoring the intuitive side of us, leaves us struggling with the simplest of tasks or robs us of making confident decisions. We then find us just going through the motions of living, instead of being fully in our lives, embracing the challenges or opportunities in order to succeed.

Through life's negative experiences we take the risk of falling out of love with us, and the process of getting our lives back on track becomes hard work. We quite often become disheartened as we withdraw more and more from our truth and true self, all because we didn't listen to that small voice within. We then find ourselves losing sight of our self belief, faith or trust in us, and our lives become harder and harder, has what we want to achieve just keeps eluding us.

Our intuition is our true-self speaking to us, guiding us naturally through life's experiences, good or bad. When something bad is looming our gut reaction kicks in, with us instantly knowing that danger is lurking or we're just about to make a big mistake! But then depending on our insecurities or emotional needs, we move forwards regardless of the consequence, and then risk becoming disheartened even more because our efforts ended in failure or not as we hoped for!

We owe it to us to listen to our intuition, because no one knows better than we do, about what's right or wrong for us. This is our truth! So to be self aware is to listen and act on our truth, knowing instantly what our truth is, and understanding that our truth is not necessarily someone else's truth. We are

14

all evolving at different times and at different levels. This is why we must be tolerant and kind to us and others, and not to judge, because we are all working to our own hidden agenda's of our life's purpose, and lessons.

When we listen to our intuitive self, we are listening to our higher conscious self, which allows us to sort our lives out consciously. The more we act on our intuitive impulses the more we get right, and the more knowing we then become. Within the blueprint of us, is all that we need to know, in order to help us and others, evolve successfully. This is when we truly show compassion, because if we accept our learning's as part of life's experiences, we'll know that no one is right or wrong. We are all trying to live our lives to the best of our abilities and in truth, even though our levels of truth change as we change. We are constantly influenced by the different aspects of our life's purpose or lessons, in order to understand what's expected from us.

The Age of Aquarius is about us all becoming our truth, and activating our intuition and intuitive skills, with us realising our abilities and limitless potential in order to help humankind. We have to help us first and foremost, and then we're able to help others successfully without any cost to us. What we give out, we will get back, but only if we give from the heart with pure joy and pleasure, of offering service to another. Everything we do as to be of purest intention, and with no hidden agenda. Self awareness is to know who we really are, and that of our capabilities or potential. We can empower us to be whatever we want to be, good or bad; so be careful what you wish for, because we all have the power of manifestation within us.

Manifestation is projecting our thoughts out into the universe in order for our dreams or goals to become a reality, so it's important to only have positive thoughts or intention. Projection of our thoughts is to manifest our desires or dreams, and by sending then out into the universe we are making our intentions of what we want to accomplish a

15

vibrational force, in order for us to manifest them successfully. With purposeful action and intention, our dreams or goals come into fruition, with many other opportunities presenting themselves to us, but we must be able to recognise and seize them, in order to succeed.

When we send our negative thoughts into the universe they will also manifest, so be careful of what you wish for. Self awareness is being self aware to our many needs, sometimes we wish for things that we don't really want or have not given enough thought to the outcome or purpose. Self awareness is to have a responsibility to the self, and all that we do should be with the greatest of intention for all. We must hold the vision of what we want to accomplish until we've achieved them, regardless of any set back or outside influence.

When progressing on our journey of self awareness will re-ignite self love, with us being really proud of us and our achievements. We have to treat us like we would our best friend, and we need to love us enough to say no to the demands of others. When we achieve self-love, we ignite self-belief; because we have to believe in us even when the odds are against us. With determination and conviction, we should see our dreams and goals through to completion. This gives us self-trust, we have to trust ourselves to complete our tasks or promises, and have commitment to achieving them, as well as a positive outcome for all. The more successful we are, the more self-faith we have. We need complete faith in us and our abilities, in order to achieve our dreams, visions or goals, irrespectively of any outside pressures or influences.

Self awareness is to have self-love, belief, faith and trust in us, first and foremost, and to have them in the universal energy of our creator, knowing instinctively that what we need will be provided for. When we listen to our intuitiveness we are listening to our higher conscious self, the infinite power within us, and the collective consciousness of the ascended us. This power allows us to achieve health, wealth, and happiness, within all aspects of our lives naturally.

When our bodies start to break down, and illness or disease becomes a problem to us, it's about us realising that we have strayed away from the power within of our higher conscious and collective self. Our infinite power within, helps us to administer self healing, and allows us to recognise the disharmonious situation within. With our new found awareness of us and all things, alters our state of perception which allows us to be accepting of all things good or bad, this brings about an instant healing to the imbalances within.

To be self-aware is to acknowledge sooner rather than later that we need help, because if we take action straight away, there is nothing that we can't overcome with foresight and understanding. When listening to our intuitiveness it will lead us away from danger, and not into it. Our gifts, skills and abilities are our natural talent within, they allow us to see or recognise the truth of any given situation or circumstance. Our emotions are positive responses to what is going on within our everyday lives, and also within our mind, body or soul. To be self aware of our will allow us to maintain health on all levels of existence, which has a huge impact on all that we do.

Our journey of self awareness is about the self-discovery of our authentic-self, truth, and infinite power within us. The Age of Aquarius is about us all reconnecting with the infinite power within, reinstating the life that was intended long ago. We all travel our life's journey, driven by the quest of our soul whilst in search of our own personal truth. The truth resides within; all we have to do is recognise our truth, as we experience the different aspects of our life's purpose or lessons. We must embrace the journey of the self; back to our higher conscious self, helping us to transforms our lives from the realms of our lower conscious living.

Self awareness is to be aware of living our lives consciously, has we embrace the transition of the human race in the purification and cleansing of the mind, body, and soul. We will also take an active part in the purification and cleansing of the earth and its structure, and every living thing that resides upon our planet!

Purification and cleansing of the mind, is to let go of the restraints and restrictions that we hold us too, but also to let go of the controls that stop us from going with the flow of life naturally. When we do this we'll start to live our lives in the now, with us becoming more accepting of the different situation or circumstances within our lives. We need to let go of any mental exhaustion, pressure or overload from our negative thoughts or worries, because when we live in fear of what may happen to us, it stops us from living our lives to the best of our abilities.

The purification and cleansing of our body, is to let go of the anguish, heartache, resentment, regrets, rejection or trauma. In fact any negative emotions or issues that we've held onto through fear or our insecurities, all because we'd not processed our negative emotions properly. By not accepting what happens to us, we're not able to find a positive solution to the disharmonious situation or circumstances. We need to let go of the imbalances that are held within, by recognising where we've stored the imbalance, illness or disease, and then set about eradicating it from within us and our lives.

We need to understand why we have an ailment or condition in the first place, and by addressing our negative emotions that's associated with it, allows us to understand what's happened or happening, in order to overcome them. When we're not truthful with us about any situation or circumstance that we find us in, it's because of our need for self preservation which overrides our positive thoughts, creating the illusions or unrest within. We need to go through the purification and cleansing process, in order to eradicate disease or illness from within. We all have the ability to self-heal, and also to heal others less fortunate than us, by helping them to understand and heal the different aspects of their lives.

Once we achieved the purification and cleansing of our minds, body and soul, allows us to lead a more spiritual life. When we become spiritual, we become spiritually aware of our many needs and those of others, granting us a higher vibrational level of existence. To be spiritually aware means to gain the unique understanding of what we cannot see or feel but sense, enabling us to recognise the unrest within as it happens. This allows us to acknowledge the life changing experiences of the unknown fearlessly. The unknown is known to us but on a higher vibrational level, and when we become all knowing it's our higher conscious and ascended self, inspiring and guiding us, through our life's quest.

When we have completed the journey of being self-aware it reinstates our natural gifts, skills and abilities naturally, allowing us to achieve things beyond our wildest dreams. We then stand more chance of recognising or reaching our potential, realising that's its limitless. This process allows us to pursue the next level of personal and spiritual growth, knowing that we have the rest of our lives in order to experience all aspects of our spirituality and earthly existence.

Our truth is our higher conscious self; and our power is being our higher conscious self at all times. Our limitless potential is being our ascended self, and the ascended self knows no boundaries. Everything within our lives become all encompassing, and all that we need to know is achieved by tapping into the collective consciousness of us, humankind and all of creation.

A JOURNEY OF TRUTH

When we recognise what is wrong within our lives, we can then take positive action, with us trying to understand what our problems are all about. We need to recognise our hidden agenda's behind what we do, say or think, because our actions are not always about our truth, but about self-preservation or our survival instincts. We all do things within our lives, not always recognising our ulterior motive. We feel at times that we do not have a choice as to what happens to us, but the truth is, we always have a choice, and by feeling that we don't is just our perception of us evading the truth. By not recognising our truth, our problems continue and at times spiral out of control, leaving us struggling with the simplest of tasks.

If we put our hand over our hearts, and ask ourselves am I doing this, that or the other for the right reasons? With practice you would feel a response from your hearts energy. This response can be a negative or positive, and with the technique of being body-aware you'll get an instant response of swaying forwards for a positive response, and backwards for a negative response. If we do things for the wrong reasons we find ourselves justifying our actions, taking the risk of them back firing on us. Our negative emotions will then affect us in many ways, and at times having an adverse effect on our health, which left untreated, will eventually influence, and compromise our happiness or well being state long term.

What is our TRUTH? Our truth is behind our thoughts, hidden agenda and deeds; our truth is also the engine of the body, mind and soul that propels us forwards in life, in search of the truth. The truth is the power behind our actions, interactions, and our relationship with us and others, as well as with all things. Our truth is the history of whom we have ever been, and to what we have done or accomplished, and it's contains all details about this pre-agreed life, and of past lifetimes too. So this life is about searching for our personal truth, in order to live our lives successfully, with us reinventing and rediscovering our authentic self once more.

We often create illusions within our lives whilst trying to understand our level of truth, so we can cope with what's happening to us, and to feel good about what we're doing. At times we justify our actions, whether it's for us or someone else just to make the situation or circumstance feel right. When we are honest with us about what we're doing, and by altering our perception to what's happening, can have a positive effect on us, and the situation or circumstances within our lives. This process creates a more successful outcome to any endeavour, and for all concerned by simply recognising our truth.

I have listed some illusions that we often create for us unknowingly.

We can often give up of ourselves to help others, when in-fact our needs are greater, maybe focusing on them means we do not have to focus on us.

We project our love onto others at a time when we don't love or even like us anymore, maybe feeling unloved.

We say we are alright when in-fact we are not, denying ourselves contact or affection from others which makes us feel lonely or unsupported.

We get angry with others when in-fact we are angry at ourselves, all because we're not being honest with us and we hadn't recognised why we're angry?

We feel we are being punished in some-way, when we're punishing the self. Often beating us up over things that we'd thought we had got wrong or for not achieving our dreams, when we'd made a promise to us to do so.

We say we are not bothered by some situation or other, when in-fact we are!

We say yes to things when we mean no! At times we don't love ourselves enough in order to say no to the demands of others.

We deny ourselves of things because we think we are not worthy or deserving in some-way.

We self-doubt, then end up giving our power away to someone else, thinking they know better or we make them more important than us.

We project our insecurities onto others, which then allow us to feel secure when we're not, leaving us feeling despondent or frustrated.

We put restrictions within our life, when we are fearful about moving forwards.

We stop believing in us because we have lost inner faith, belief or trust, in us and the process of life.

We feel threaten by the choices or decisions made by others, because we are afraid to make our own.

We feel lonely and depressed because we no longer take responsibility for us or we've given up on ourselves.

We are never betrayed unless we have betrayed ourselves first, by not living the life that was intended, instead of the one created from our insecurities.

We often experience a lack of trust, faith, belief, and love for ourselves, which causes us to disconnect from our higher conscious self, and that of our truth.

Procrastination of the self, will eventually lead to blaming others for the things that are wrong within our lives. With us thinking that we did not have a choice to what's happening to us, so we just went along with it in a blind fog! With us not being able to see a way out or find a solution to our problems.

Procrastination of the self can lead to falling out of love with the self and others or even our creator as we look for something or someone to blame for what's happened!

Our negative emotions are positive emotions as long as we acknowledge them, and then take action to alleviating the negativity before it has chance to lock into our sub conscious mind. Negative issues can very easily become a negative program or belief, influencing our lives which leave us struggling or frustrated.

When we are not fully in our lives we just go through the process of living in the past or the future, but not in the present time! We then waste or bide our time until things get better but take a huge risk that they never will. Or we can take positive action, and by changing our mindset of how we perceived the different aspects within our lives, we can then embrace change.

When we reinstate equilibrium between the mind, body, and soul, we reconnect with the universal life-force energy that sustains all growth, whether it's physically, mentally, emotionally or spiritually. This guarantees us with continued success in all areas of our lives, allowing us to achieve our dreams, goals and visions. So once we recognise the imbalances within, we can introduce a new thought process that allows us to become positive in the decisions we then make. We need to recognise, and seize the many opportunities as they present themselves to us, knowing with confidence that they're the small steps we need to take, in order to realise and reach our limitless potential.

We also need to realise that we are already living part of our dreams or ambitions, and this process will allow us to be living our lives successfully in the NOW! Accomplishing what we want today, instead of putting our dreams or ambitions off until tomorrow, with us taking the risk that we'll never accomplish them.

The secret is to understand what the real reason is behind what we do, re-addressing any negative issues that present themselves to us or within our lives. We must make sure that our actions are about our truth, and it's important to recognise the imbalances within, because sometimes we do things from feeling insecure, unhappy or that we're bored with our lives or us. When we realise this, we stand more chance of turning a negative issue or problem into a positive action and outcome.

When I wanted to understand my negative situation or circumstance, I would get a worksheet and write down why I felt blocked or depressed. I would try to understand the negative emotion within by trying to be honest with myself as to what was really going on. For example if I was feeling lonely I would try to understand what part of me felt this, maybe it was just a lack of support or maybe I felt let down by others not being there for me, when I'd been there for them!

The solution to the problem was? I was not open to that support because I felt lonely and I'd closed myself down by protecting me, all because I felt forgotten about and that it was never my turn. We often use others or the different situations as blame, justifying why we feel we cannot achieve the different things that we wanted to accomplish. So once we've recognised the fact that we're blocking us or self sabotaging our efforts, and that it's not someone or something else, we can then start the process of finding a positive solution to releasing the imbalances from within. Once we've done this we need to replace the negative imbalance, with a positive empowered affirmation or statement that would empower and lead us to SUCCESS, in all we do.

My empowered affirmation was:

I realise my full potential and it's safe for me to be fully in my life now. I am totally supported by the universe and everyone, and I am open to that support now. I am safe and secure and trust in the process of my life.

When I felt blocked in my decisions to get my first book published and start a new career, I often heard myself saying "I can't get my book published because I have no money." When I had some money, guess what! I still didn't get my book published, it was only when I'd addressed the emotional issues within that I found I had a fear of failure. The fear was because I'd thought I'd already failed with the different situation and circumstances that had happened to me. I also had a fear of living, feeling that I'd achieved it once and had it all taken away, so why should I have to do it all over again, life at times seemed so unfair? Only on releasing the old belief's and replacing it with positive belief's could I succeed, turning my life around, not just publishing one book but now on my fifth.

My empowered affirmation was:

I am willing to forgive the past and rejoice in my infinite knowledge and wisdom, and it's safe for me to go beyond my limitations now.

There are lots of ways of realising the negative issues within, but we need to find the more lasting approaches as opposed to the quick fixes. It is the journey of the soul, the self back to self, and the reconnection to our true inner-self, which aids us with the crossing over from the lower conscious self, to the higher conscious self.

It's important that we maintain a positive attitude to our new thought process, so I would place my chosen affirmation that I'd written onto a piece of paper and attached it to my dressing table mirror, where I could continue to recite the affirmation daily for one week, in order to empowered my mind, body, and soul completely. Also as a reminder to me of the promise I'd now made, because affirmations are the promises we make to us to change our lives positively, and consciously.

I have been on my spiritual pathway for over thirty years, and I have found the only true way to reconnect with your higher conscious self is working directly with your own infinite energy and higher consciousness. We can reconnect to our higher conscious self and that of the universal energy of our creator just by simply placing our hand over the heart and allowing our minds energy to go within. This will instantly connect us to our infinite power, and it's an exercise that we can do anywhere, and at any-time. We are the co-creation of pure energy; all that we need is within and provided for by our creator, so just connect with it, because it's our infinite healing energy of our higher conscious self.

We must make sure we are open to receiving in order to actually receive what we need. If we're closed to receiving help in anyway, it's because we feel un-worthy or doubting of ourselves which blocks us from receiving the help that we so desperately need. We often struggle with the different aspects within our lives, maybe we've self destructed or self sabotaged our efforts, only making an indifferent effort because we feel we've already failed. This is a process that goes on until we realise how we've been blocking us through our fears, insecurities, negative emotions, beliefs or programs.

We often display feelings such as resentment, regret or rejection which disables us from being in control of our every-lives, and stops us from achieving our dreams because we're not going with the flow of life. We then find us struggling, giving up on our dreams or goals when they are just in-sight. It's a continual battle of heartache, and disappointment which breads discontent and unhappiness, and leaves us feeling unfulfilled.

When understanding that we're unique in every-way, and all that we need is within, just waiting for us to reconnect with

27

but when we're ready too. We will then automatically connect to our definitive power of conviction and intention, with us instinctively knowing our true direction ion life. We often find ourselves travelling the universe and back again, in search for the infinite knowledge and wisdom that would set us free. Not realising that it's within our hearts and soul, just waiting for us to reconnect with once more. This reconnection of our higher conscious us and would enable us to reinvent, and rediscover our authentic selves, and that of our personal and spiritual truth. This connection brings about an infinite healing of the mind, body and soul, allowing us to be our truth naturally and at all times.

The Age of Aquarius brings new beginning for us all, but first we must let go of our negative emotions and traits. With this new age comes the clearing of the sub-conscious and conscious mind, of our repressed emotional issues. Once released, we can reconnect to our higher consciousness allowing us to become a part of the collective consciousness of mankind. It is important that we reconnect with our personal inner resources in order to meet, and overcome all of life's challenges transforming our lives consciously.

It takes courage to participate in the soul's journey, and quest that enables us to reconnect with the ultimate power of our truth. This journey reveals the real reasons behind why the different situations or circumstances have happened to us, all being a part of our life's path, and the experiences that we need in order for us to evolve successfully. This process allows us to reconnect with our instinctive and intuitive impulses that we need to recognise, and act upon in order to allow our lives to change naturally. These life changing situations allow us to take back the control of our true destiny, so we can achieve our dreams, and fulfil our mission in life.

Over the next few years we're all going to experience some very hard times, we may even be experiencing them now. It's important that we get our lives back on-track, and overcome our problems which would allow our vibrations to naturally evolve from a fourth dimensional being, to a fifth or maybe a sixth dimensional being. This would enable us to naturally become our higher consciousness, with us using our gifts, skills and abilities instinctively. This allows us to attract positive situations to us, in order to manifest all of our dreams, desires, and ambitions effortlessly. But first we must overcome any problem or lesson successfully, accepting all things that's happened to us as part of our life path and purpose, and part of the divine plan.

At the present time we are all questioning what is happening to us and our world, with many changes that we're being forced to go through. We are experiencing natural disasters as the earth is going through its own purification and cleansing process, with catastrophic changes to our planet and individuals. How do we survive a tsunami and the total devastation to lives? The only sure way is to reconnect with our infinite power, in order to know the truth of all things, and accessing our natural survival instincts that would lead us away from danger and not into it.

So what does the future hold? The Age of Aquarius is upon us, and it demands codes of conduct from us all, along with the responsibility to us, too evoke positive change. With each evolutionary age, come the different trends and cycles. This new age we have us all experiencing lots of changes, some of which will not be pleasant, but whatever happens we should be prepared for it.

The Age of Aquarius encourages us to be self-aware, spiritually-aware, and consciously-aware of all things. The twenty first century has new beginnings for us all, but first we must let go of the old ways of thinking and doing. This process will free us to embrace the golden age of opportunity and growth, on all levels of existence. We have to eradicate human suffering, and encourage each individual to seek inner peace with us eventually achieving world peace.

We will experience the earth energy changing which will have a huge effect on each individual's energy, with our physical bodies and minds, being influenced by the corresponding effects of the earth, and the solar systems energy, all due to the weakening of the magnetic field. We need to allow our vibrations to evolve in order to cope with these changes that are hypothetically being forced upon us. These changes will allow us all the opportunity of not being left behind to suffer needlessly; we need to embrace this transformational period of great phenomenon, and participated in the spiritual reawakening of our world and our souls, once more.

We are re-cycled souls, time travellers who are aiming to undo all that we've done or perceived wrongly in the past, and over many centuries which have added to our present climate, and the slow decline of our planet and ourselves. We have brought this all on by our constant needs and wants, adding to the demands made upon our natural resources that affect us greatly.

Our planet is meant to have natural disasters because it's slowly claiming back its true origin, an evolutionary cycle with extinction being a natural part of the earth's journey to rest in order to regenerate. This process restores balance and harmony, really no different to us and our soul, as we need to undo what we've done to us over the many centuries, as well as within this lifetime. Only then can we become whole and complete once more, and live our lives as it was intended.

We need to tap into the collective consciousness of mankind in order to rid our world of the mass negativity. So by playing our individual and conscious part in this evolutionary transformation, will give us all we need to live abundantly within our chosen lifestyles, and within the structure of our world. Miracles do happen! But first we need to reconnect with this evolutionary power of the creator that's within us all, and perform our own miracles by healing our lives, and that of others, and that's the truth!

30

THE SOUL'S PURPOSE

We came into this lifetime having already pre-agreed to the different situations and circumstances that would happen to us, all part of our life's purpose and plan. The palms of our hands have the details in-printed on them, and hold the secrets of our inherited characteristics, and our personalities, unique talents, abilities, and the different aspects of our genetic identification. Our palms also hold the important events and times within our lives, in-fact everything we need to know about us in order to evolve successfully through this pre-agreed lifetime, and to the best of our ability.

Our hand gestures tell us a lot about what is going on within our lives, almost on a daily basis. They also tell us a lot about what going on within us, has our hand gestures change as we alter our perception about the different things that are or have happened to us. A person who is considered to be a balanced person, their hand gestures would be natural with their fingers being evenly displayed as they waved their hands around. A person with personal problems, their fingers would be out of line, with gaps between each finger which represents the details of life. These details differ between each individual because of our life's experiences, but never the less tells us a lot about what going on within our lives.

We are identified by our fingerprints which are unique to every individual; no two sets of fingerprints are the same, which makes us unique in every-way. We all have different hidden agendas that we are working too. So it's important that we do not judge others or ourselves, because we haven't fully understood the truth about our existence of this lifetime, let alone other lifetimes. So once we've recognised, and understood our life's purpose and lessons, we stand more of a chance of realising and reaching our limitless potential. We need to help and encourage others less fortunate than us, to find and reach their unrealised potential too.

Once we understand these important aspects of us, we stand more chance of seeing the bigger picture of our lives, realising how everything and everyone is interconnected. By showing love and compassion, and being tolerant and kind to one another, would save us all from a lot of uncertainty which creates the negativity that causes us pain or grief. This happens because we have judged one another unnecessarily, instead of being more accepting of each other. We are all right in what we do, because we're working to our own agenda's. We just consider each other to be wrong, because of our lack of understanding. Why else would we do what we do, unless each individual thought they were right? Hypothetically, we are all being influenced by our hidden agenda's of our life's purpose or lessons with us gaining experience.

The decisions we make our based on aspects of our truth, and every body's individual truth is different. To maintain balance within our lives is to recognise that no-one is made to do anything that they didn't want to do, as everything happens for a reason. It's just that we are not always privy to the real truth behind the reasons. They say, what goes around, comes around, and my experience is that in previous lives we have done it all, good or bad. What happened to me within this lifetime I had created for someone else in another lifetime, so I had a karmic debt to pay back? So if we can just be more accepting of what is happening to us, would save us from a lot of pain and grief, or the disharmonious situations, and unhappiness that we attract at times.

Our destiny is what we make it. We all have the potential of great things but first we need to claim back the control of our true destiny, by reconnecting to our true-selves and that of our truth once more. Remember the truth is behind the power of our actions or did we find ourselves justifying our actions, maybe out of sense of guilt or even that of the pride and ego? We have an obligation to us, to speak our truth, hear our truth, and see our truth, at all times. We all have choices to make, but it's important to make those choices for ourselves first and foremost, because we are the most important person in our life, and it's important to look after us.

How many times have you heard yourself say or others that they had no choice. The fact is, we do have a choice, we can say yes or no! We have to give to ourselves first, before we're in a position to give to others successfully. It's about not giving up of us because of the demands of others or even of our own expectations being too high. To claim back our true destiny is about claiming back our birthright and place to be, within the family of life. We must know that we're important too and by recognising that we must put us first, with us being worthy of success that allows us then, to help others less fortunate than us.

It's important to give ourselves the permission to get our lives back on track, and only accept the best that life can offer, in order to become successful in all that we do. This allows us to help others successfully, all because we're a balanced person that doesn't feel threatened by the demands of others. This allows us to be supportive, and to encourage others to do the same, without us making unnecessarily demands on each other, when we all want, is to succeed in fulfilling our dreams or goals.

Our inner journey began a long time ago and it's a very exciting time, has we evolve and grow, with others naturally following. Actions speak louder than words, sometimes finding ourselves doing things instinctively, our reactions becoming natural to us, we often say things to others wondering where those words of wisdom came from? Everything we need is within us, and provided for by the universe. It's important that we become more conscious-aware, recognising the many synchronicities and coincidences within our lives. This is the collective consciousness of the universe, giving us the many opportunities needed in understanding our problems then allowing us access to the solutions in order to solve them.

Everything that happens to us happens for a reason, for nothing is by chance, it's all part of the divine and universal plan, and life's great adventure in helping us all, overcome our life's purpose and lessons. The soul's quest is ongoing and through many lifetimes. Within each lifetime, we must reinvent and rediscover our authentic self, allowing us to empower ourselves, transforming our lives consciously and in so many different ways.

We hypothetically travel the universe and back again, in search of our truth, with us achieving and experiencing many things. Our truth is hidden deep within us, just waiting for the right time for us to reconnect with, where we'll reawaken to our dreams and desires, realising that all the steps that we've already taken, has taken us closer to achieving those dreams. It's important to enjoy the process of striving towards living our dreams or desires, as all the different aspects that we experience is all part of the process. This enables us to accomplish our goals easily whilst gaining valuable knowledge, which gives us infinite wisdom.

In acceptance in all that we do, will make us feel more secure and confident, about the decisions that we make, instead of us chasing rainbows for the pot of gold at the end of it. It's recognising what we've already have within our lives, showing gratitude for the things that we hold so dear. Just stop to think of those less fortunate than yourself, and you'll realise just how lucky you really are.

I feel that the future holds great things for us all, but first we have to let go of the negativity and blocks within our lives, that stops us from achieving our goals. When all is said and done, it is up to us to readjust if things are not as we want or like. We have freedom to choose, but first we must recognise that fact, and then we can move forwards with confidence has our soul gently leads us through life's learning's with guidance and inspiration.

This is our life, and we must have the star role within it. It's no dress rehearsal, we get just one shot at getting it right because if we don't, we have to come back into another lifetime, and do it all over again. It would be another life with different situations and circumstances in order for us to try and learn from, but let's do us a favour by getting it right this time around. Who knows the next lifetime that we have could be a lot easier than this one, with us enjoying all that we do, joyfully and blissfully. More importantly a life where we could use our inherited gifts, skills and abilities, our mystical talents that would allow us to achieve health, wealth and happiness on all levels of existence, but naturally.

Our destiny is our responsibility, and we have to take back the controls of our life in a positive and decisive manner. By reprogramming our minds, the body will respond in a positive and accepting way. We can then choose how we deal with the negativity that we're exposed ourselves too, so it doesn't affect our bodies or minds. Confidently knowing that we can turn any negative situation or circumstance, into a positive understanding and lesson learned, with us fulfilling our soul's quest.

The transformation from the lower conscious self to the higher conscious self is quite profound. It changes our lives forever, the transformation is noticeable to everyone around us; our whole persona will look more vibrant, rejuvenating the body, mind and soul. This will enhance our sense of survival, a willingness to become our true self, whilst experiencing our power of divinity. This creates an inner peace that aids in maintaining a youthful body and mind, and allowing us to unleash our creativity, artistic skills, and talents.

Enlightened is who we become, when we've achieved the reconnection with our higher consciousness. The enlightened state of awareness is about the in-sight into the vision of the life that our creator intended for us all to experience. Only then would we truly be living our lives to the full, achieving contentment and fulfilment in all that we do. We

35

would then become a part of the collective consciousness of mankind again, where we could achieve enlightenment, our natural power of divinity. Our vibrations vibrating at a level where the world's mass-negativity would become neutralised, and we could eventually achieved inner and world peace.

When we empower ourselves with positive affirmations aids us to become successful in all we do, achieving our dreams or goals consciously. Empowered affirmations reignite our sub-conscious into conscious thinking and action. We empower us even though we sometimes self-doubt or have a lack of self-belief, faith or trust in us, knowing that we can instantly rectify the imbalances that we create through outside influences.

The power of positive affirmations or commands has a profound effect on the mind, body and soul. We can empower our perception by being our truth at all times, making us more accepting to what has happened to us, good or bad. When we recite positive affirmations, and connect with our higher conscious self allows us to re-educate us into becoming more self-aware, spiritually-aware, and when we listen to our bodies many needs, we become more body-aware. This allows us to continue our evolutionary journey into the unknown of the 21st century, and The Golden Age of Aquarius; this is the age of potential and prosperity but more importantly we will be the crusaders of truth.

We are now living in The Golden Age of Aquarius, and the world did not end on 21st December 2012 but carried on regardless of the publicity and ancient prophecies. We must open ourselves up to the prospects of great possibilities and opportunities, has we embrace positive growth and change. At this present time we are all questioning what is to happen in the near and distant future, because we all find the prospects of our future very daunting at times.

The only sure thing that we can change is our perception and attitude of how we are going to deal with the current state of affairs. They say that everything happens for a reason, so what is it all about? It's in order for us to understand what our life's purpose is all about, and we do this by embracing the present time by being our higher conscious self. We must try to the best of our ability in order to fulfil the quest of our soul's purpose, in achieving a successful and healthy life effortlessly.

In understanding the dramatic climate changes, and natural disasters such as earthquakes, volcanoes erupting, and worldwide flooding which leaves us with devastation, and disruption to our everyday lives, knowing its all part of evolution. Over the next few years, we will continue to see a lot of natural catastrophic changes to our planet, with us all having to adjust. These natural disasters are about the cleansing and purification of our planet, also with a spiritual transition period of the purification and cleansing of humankind.

Within the blueprint of us, is a knowing of what's to happen, and what the future holds for us all, because this is the soul's quest. We must allow our hearts it full potential to love unconditionally including ourselves. To be fearless and not afraid to break new ground, allowing our lives to naturally move on, through the transitions that we must experience, all being a part of our soul's purpose and quest. We must have the ability to take direct and correct action on intuitive impulses, in order to achieve all we desire naturally.

We must try not to panic as we are being made aware of these natural changes that we all need to make in order to continue our life on earth. The part that we play is in realising that we need to take responsibility for us and what we do, and do whatever it takes to get our lives back on track. The empowered affirmations are just one way of achieving it consciously. So I hope you enjoy the experience and journey?

THE GOLDEN AGE

The Golden Age of Aquarius, last approximately for 2,150 years. We are now living in the age of great potential which promotes, and reignites the spiritual reawakening of each individual. Enlightened spirituality is the rising of the collective consciousness to heal a wounded world, and our souls. New beginnings are often disguised as painful endings as we lift the veils of our painful deceptions of the illusions we've created, all because of the ignorance of our disconnection from our higher conscious self. It's important that we embrace change within our lives, all being a natural part of our continued growth and survival of us, within a world where there is so much unrest.

We must all try to focus and reconnect to the energy of our higher consciousness in order to let go of the old ways of doing and perceiving, which will allow us to embrace a better future. We do this by participating in this golden age of limitless potential, personal and spiritual growth. Once we realise that we no longer need to fight for survival, but by embracing this new beginning, we can evoke a new and better world. Awakening comes from suffering, but only if we choose to suffer no longer, we can then achieve a brighter future for us, and future generations.

The journey of the lower conscious self promotes suffering and keeps us fearful; this prevents us from attaining a positive future. Our focus is on the material world which keeps us locked into the illusions of being happy when the unrest of our soul is still very evident within us. This leaves us struggling to achieve a well being state, which can affect our health, wealth or happiness, has we continue to struggle with the different aspects of our lives.

The journey of the higher conscious self allows us to alleviate our suffering, which then gives us courage to achieve a better future not just for us, but everyone. The reawakening of our true-self allows us to lift the veil of illusion or deceit, and allows us to explore the rebirth of our higher conscious self. We can become anything we want, achieving all that we desire by allowing us to become our limitless potential of our past lives. The memories of which is stored deep within our sub-conscious, memories of some forgotten time of our accomplishments and achievements, just waiting for us to reactivate, and use once more in order to enhance all lives.

This is the age of the reawakening of our infinite knowledge and wisdom, and unique gifts, skills and abilities which aid us in healing our lives. We must take responsibility for us and our well being, and by embracing the opportunities that waits us, will allow us to achieve our goals during the transition of the reawakening of our authentic selves. Our authentic self is our truest form and origin, and by integrating with our authenticity, allows us to become a powerful human being once more.

The Phoenix rises from the ashes of the old self, every 2,000 years. The Age of Aquarius is the rising of the new us as we embrace this golden age from the ashes of the old us, and our world. Evolution is to re-educate us to become our genius self, with the reactivation of our gifts, skills and abilities which makes us all unique individuals. We must all strive for better times whilst being driven by our infinite power of conviction, courage and intention, from within.

The spiritual awakening of our world will have us all using more of our brain capacity and hearts energy, and with the awakening of our pineal gland comes the upgrade of our DNA. We will all eventually be using parts of our brains that have been dormant for thousands of years; spiritual awakening will allow us to activate our Astral Bodies, and to be at one with the greater us. It's important that we ascend our earthly limitations, with us achieving things beyond our wildest imagination or dreams. We'll reach new levels of existence, whilst living our lives in our human form, instead of ascending after death in order to understand what our life on earth was all about. This phenomenon can now happen on the astral plane whilst we're living our earthly lives, and just by being our higher conscious self, will allow us to become our ascended selves, through the transition of enlightened awareness.

The Golden Age of potential will have us all going through a series of initiations and transitions. The starting point is with the self, and a willingness to change allows us to experience a correct relationship with the self, with us being yielding, devoted, and to know our true direction in life. This is a time of major growth, and rectification must come before progress. It's the purification and cleansing of the conscious and sub conscious mind, with us reflecting on every aspect of our lives. We must evoke self-change by letting go of attachments to beliefs, programming, our expectations or standards, in fact anything that we hold us too, that create the restraints or restrictions within our lives.

We need nourishment and nurture to move into an enlightened state, we must take responsibility for us and our actions, whilst encouraging beneficial outcomes for all. We must apply conviction to our efforts, and cultivate our choices or decisions with care, being realistic in the goals or tasks we set ourselves. With a strong will and through positive action we must stay unattached to the outcome, remaining mindful of the importance of being patience. When we go with the flow of life, we make steady progress whilst allowing us to be more accepting of all situations. This process allows all things to happen naturally, and within the timing of the divine plan.

The initiation of the liberation from the old self, to the new self, will give us freedom from the old ways of doing and perceiving. This process evokes the great awakener of our higher consciousness, and a deep level of transformation and recognition of our truth. The initiation process of letting go of the past and embracing the now, allows us to plan for a future of great potential, with us activating our truth at all times.

41

Our higher conscious self is who we really are, and not the lower conscious us that's affected the different aspects of our lives because of the hardships and suffering, created from our insecurities or negative beliefs. Our higher conscious us, will have us moving forwards with confidence and conviction. It's important that we do not buy into the negativity that surrounds us almost daily, and affects our lives continually. By rising above the uncertainty, and not letting the things that we have no control over to affect us, will have us solving problems, instead of becoming a part of them.

Only good comes from all of life's experiences, but we have to be open to understanding them. With all negative situations there is a positive learning, and we have a choice in how we deal with these negative situations, and to how they affect us. We have to trust in the positive unfolding of our lives, and our higher conscious us will enable us, to do just that. Our natural resources of the higher self will have us embracing this golden age with compassion, and understanding of all situations, others, and even ourselves.

We all have the ability to heal our lives, and empower us to succeed. Positive thoughts and action, promotes positive growth, and guarantees us with a positive future. Being truthful to us about what's going on within our lives, will have us fulfilling our commitment to our soul, and that is to live our lives to the full, and be prosperous in all we do.

We all need to show gratitude for all we have within our lives, and to know and embrace the higher conscious us, as well as our achievements and accomplishments. The recognition of self-belief, faith and trust in us, promotes self love which allows us to embrace the collective consciousness of our uniqueness. This is the power of our true self, and aids in unleashing our limitless potential of all lifetimes, since time began.

Our potential is our dreams and desires of what we want to accomplish within this lifetime. With realistic steps and focus, we can achieve things beyond our wildest dreams as long as we have courage and conviction to go beyond our limitations. The golden age of opportunity will have us all acknowledging our true vocations in life, with us instantly recognising our soul-mates or infinitive souls that will enhance our lives, and us theirs.

Spirituality as just one purpose, for it's not just a way of life but the journey of recognising our authentic selves once more, by seeing, hearing and speaking our truth. We do this by being spirituality aware of the greater us, and by embracing the truth of any situation or circumstance that we find us experiencing. When we allow the process of life to unfold naturally, allows us to succeed in all that we do. With acceptance of all situations allows us to be fully in our lives, and not just going through the process. We will instantly know that all of our needs are being taken care of, but on a higher conscious level of existence.

The power of the mind can have us all changing our lives for the better, with us realising that we don't have to buy into the negative traits of our shortfalls or doing. By accepting that everything happens for a reason, we gain the understanding of what that reason was all about!

I have been travelling my own personal journey of understanding my life's purpose for a very long time, and only now fully understanding the significance of the soul's true quest. Spirituality promotes truth by seeking the understanding of our life's experiences, and the recognition of these experiences will set us free. We make life so complicated with us pushing ourselves to the absolute limits, with us being unrealistic in the goals we've set ourselves. We often become a salve to our own standards or expectations, not realising we're being unrealistic in the tasks or goals we've set ourselves.

The Age of Aquarius allows us to perfect our goals by making us aware of our natural gifts, skills, and abilities. We must recognise their truest potential in allowing us to be the best we can be, with us embracing our infinite power of intention and conviction from within. We must naturally be willing to be true to us because its uniqueness will allow us to recognise what to do, and more importantly when to do it. The uniqueness of us allows us to naturally know, allowing us to make firm decisions based on our truth of any given situation. We then achieve our goals effortlessly, being content to just go with the flow of life, with us patiently waiting for our goals to manifest.

The golden age of potential is to recognise and act upon our truth, with the truth being the real reasons behind what we do and want. At times we need to accept that the timing may not be right or that others are not ready, and that a little more foresight and planning are needed before the things we want to accomplish come into fruition. With a positive mindset we can endeavour to achieve all that we set out to achieve, all because we have a clear mind and focus.

We cannot address our higher ideals until we feel secure at a higher conscious level, when were certain of our goals we feel safe and secure. We must have a clear conviction of the truth once the decision of what we want to accomplish has been made, which gives us clarity of vision without confusion or turmoil, with us being in our own power in order to succeed. We must draw strength, love and inspiration from the divine and the higher conscious us, to see our goals through to completion.

Our truth attain within this golden age, enables us to retain the infinite knowledge and wisdom gained from past experiences. This knowledge and wisdom will serve us well, giving us a clear vision of our future with excitement, conviction, direction and intention, ensuring that we'll succeed in all we do.

THE AFFIRMATIONS TECHNIQUE

The Empowered Affirmations Technique is designed to help those who want to understand and overcome any of their life's problems, ailments or conditions, easily and effectively. This technique can aid in rebalancing our energy within and around our bodies, and by eliminating any negative imbalance or disharmonious situation from within our lives, helps us achieve a well being state once more.

The process of this technique helps us with the realignment of the mind, body and soul, which is important in maintaining health, and by understanding the intricate workings of our physical, mental, emotional, and spiritual bodies, have a profound effect on us in maintain well being.

Our bodies' natural energy is constantly fed by the infinite energy of the universe that sustains all life. A process that allows us to accept and overcome life's experiences naturally and effortlessly, with us not adding additional trauma or anguish to us, which can affect us greatly, all because we didn't process our life's experiences positively.

We have a continuous flow of universal energy that's within and around the physical body which cleanses and purifies the organs, and our energy within each chakra centre within our physical bodies. Also we need to cleanse and purify the energy of our aura's that constantly fed by the energy from our chakra system. This energy influences the body's own immunity in providing all that we need in maintaining a healthy mind, body, and soul, whilst we achieve balance and harmony within every aspect of our everyday lives.

Throughout the process of living our lives to the best of our abilities, we would have developed weak areas within the body, where the mind obligingly stores the negative undertones of our miss-perceptions to the different situations or circumstances that happened to us. In some of us, these negative undertones have already been stored within since birth, maybe with us bringing them into this lifetime as part of our life-path experiences. These imbalances are stored within, just waiting for the time to become right or for us to have sufficiently exhausted ourselves with the constant battles of trying to make sense of our lives, before we address them.

When we do not recognise the pressures that we've placed ourselves under, life will normally intervene by giving us the opportunity to understand what we've allowed to happen to us. This happens in us understanding the lessons that we must learn from, because if we don't take notice, the more pressure or disharmony we'll take onboard, and the more our bodies' unique energy system will become depleted or blocked. These negative imbalances restrict the universal energy from flowing and pulsating throughout the body freely, which stops us from releasing the negativity from within. We need to be able to access our higher conscious energy that can only be reached if we've not created a block or imbalance within us, in the first place.

To maintain a healthy body and mind, we have to locate the problem within, and then set about releasing the negativity from within us and our energy field. When we fail to notice these imbalances or disharmony within, we begin to feel unwell, fatigued and in some cases develop ailments, illness or disease. Our bodies defence mechanism starts to break down, and our immunity becomes threatened. The body's energy system is fed by the universal energy that flows throughout the body, and allows us to release any negativity from within into mother earth, in order to be neutralized.

Throughout our physical body we have energy centres, acupuncture points, and meridian lines which are all interconnected with the organs, and they are constantly fed by the universal energy which maintains health on all levels of the mind, body and soul. It's important that when trying to sort our problems out, that we just focus within us, and go directly to the source of the problem or the negative emotion, regardless of any outside influence or pressure. This will allow us to gain a deeper understanding as to why we have a problem, which enables us to clear the negativity or block successfully.

The thymus is the main organ within the body that is affected through stress, the second is the heart because we take things to heart, especially if we feel we have failed in some-way or have put ourselves under too much pressure. Hard work never killed anybody, it's the way we allow our bodies and mind to respond or perceive that stress that's the number one killer. The pressures we put ourselves under, can cause us to lose touch with the simple pleasures of living a life effortlessly. This happens because we'd not recognised the disharmony within which we've allowed to become a condition or situation that now needs attention.

We often find that our lives have become serious and stressful, with us realising we've taken on too much, putting ourselves under too much pressure by being unrealistic in our goals. The thing is we're not even sure of when or how it happened but we feel the pressures, and it's begun to take its toll on us! This happens all because we've allowed our lives to be controlling us, and we don't have quality time for us anymore. Or if we did, we feel guilty at times because there are more pending things that need to be done, so we don't allow us to enjoy ourselves anymore. We sometimes leave it until it's too late, before we recognise the imbalances within, and we're forced to make life changing decisions.

When illness or disease affects are lives we then make changes, because they're forced upon us in order to achieve a well being state again, by understanding and rectifying our problems or imbalances. This happened all because we were oblivious to the fact that something was wrong or amiss. At times we kid ourselves or even pretend everything's fine, when it's not. Maybe we didn't want to upset others or our plans, when really we weren't being honest with us about what was happening and now it's taking its toll.

The secret to success is to make those life changing decisions NOW! While we're still healthy to do so, because if we leave it to late then things may happen us that would stop us from ever leading a normal and happy, healthy or contented life again. The mind plays an important part as to what happens to the physical body, mind over matter. If things really don't matter then they shouldn't affect us, but the things that do matter, affects us in lots of different ways.

We are all living within his lifetime with the intention of us over-coming issues that we'd not fully understood previously within others lifetimes, as well as this lifetime. This is our life's purpose and the lessons or experiences that we must learn from, so we can evolve successfully and achieve what we desire as we continue the journey of our soul's quest. What we do unto others, we will have done to us good or bad, what goes around comes around. This is why we must never judge, and to be honest we do not know what we've done in other incarnate lives good or bad. I believe we have done it all, but this lifetime may only be about a small proportion of those lives, and the emotional imbalances that we'd created within them.

This technique works with our higher conscious self of our soul, which resides within our heart centre. So when we place our hand over the heart it will automatically connect us to our infinite energy within. With the connection of the heart and thymus, allows them both to work in harmony, and aids us in restoring health by influencing our minds to positively deal with all negative situations or circumstances that we've experienced within our lives.

The heart connects us to our personal truth and inner spirit of our (soul), and the thymus connects us to the physical (body) and brain (mind) and with the combination of the two aids us in achieving realignment to the mind, body and soul. The universal energy influences the balancing and realignment of the mind, body and soul and by placing our hand over the heart and thymus helps us to focus on the infinite energy within. As we re-connect to this life-force energy, it will stimulate a powerful surge of universal energy that comes down through the crown chakra, and through all the other corresponding chakras, before leaving the body and into mother earth, in order to repeat the whole process again in maintaining health on all levels of existence.

The affirmations technique allows you to tap into the infinite energy whilst purifying and cleansing the mind, body and soul, this allows us to release any negative blockages or imbalances, but only once we've understood the relevance to the negativity. This process allows us, and with the use of the empowered affirmations to reprogram the mind, which then influences the body, allowing our soul to soar to a higher conscious level of existence. The body is then purified and cleansed with the continuous flow of universal energy flowing throughout our body's unique system. The more mental and physical blockages that we can remove, allows the body to respond more positively promoting well being.

When we have successfully eradicated the negativity from within, we will gain a stronger connection to our higher conscious self and that of our soul. When the mind and body has released the imbalances would enhance our lives. The physical body would then be continuously purified and cleansed by the life-force energy, as it continues to flow through the crown chakra, and all the other corresponding chakras. The energy then flows out through the base chakra into mother earth, where all negativity will be neutralised naturally.

My energy balancing experience first started about fifteen years ago, when I experienced an alternative therapy called kinesiology. This is the art of muscle testing to a direct response to a particular problem or condition. Kinesiology works with the higher consciousness and by using charts of information helps us decipher the hidden truth of our higher self, and the real reason behind our thoughts or actions. We would then administer remedies, and recite affirmations that would release the negative issues, and allowed us to achieve realignment to our physical, emotional, mental and spiritual bodies. At times when the problem was located, and with the use of the emotional freedom technique of tapping the emotional centres within the physical body or whilst working with the meridians or acupuncture points, our emotional imbalances were successfully released. This left us with us the understanding of what the condition or ailment was all about, and to what we had done to us unknowingly.

We also worked with the negativity that was stored within the different organs, also the tapping of the thymus in order to stimulate the body's own immune system because taking things to heart creates pain and grief for us. In gaining the understanding of the different organs and their association with the different corresponding energy centres, has a big effect to releasing the negativity or blocks within. All holistic techniques are about working with the higher conscious self and the universal energy of creation, the life-force-energy within and without the physical body, helping us in maintaining a well-being state on all levels of existence.

With the art of kinesiology we were able to regress to past lifetimes where we could release the negative issues associated with that particular life, and was part of our life's purpose or experiences within this life. We would then alleviate the imbalances on a deeper fundamental level which allowed us to release the negative imbalances from within the past lifetime as well as this life. This allowed us to bring forwards the positive attributes of us from any lifetime, into this life, once we'd successfully understood their relevance. These positive attributes are known as our limitless potential, the unique aspect of what we accomplished in other incarnate lives, and we can now use them within this one.

When balancing the mind, body and soul, allows the universe to work its magic, with us achieving a positive attitude to body and self awareness which promotes self healing, and allows miracles to be performed in maintaining health, wealth and happiness.

The journey of self awareness connects us to the truth of all things. The truth is hidden within, so remember the secret is to hypothetically travel the universe in search of the truth, with us experiencing our lives to the full. When the time is right, we can start our own personal journey of our soul's quest. It's a journey of a lifetime by travelling within to reconnect us to the infinite power and our truth.

It's only by consciously living our lives that we'll become aware of the imbalances or disharmony within, with us realising that what was missing from within our lives was our infinite knowledge and wisdom of our higher conscious us, and the connection to our truth.

Whatever it is that evades us or seems unobtainable, it's our responsibility to us, to reinstate it. So remember this is our life, and it's no dress rehearsal, because we are the most important person in our life. So take notice to witness our own lives first, because allowing others to take precedence over us, the only person we're deceiving is ourselves. We owe it to us to reinstate our higher conscious self, because that what's missing from within our lives and that is the truth! We have to reclaim our lives back, and take control to have the star role in our own lives, but to experience it at a higher conscious level.

This is our life, and if we get it wrong, the one to blame is us. We then risk taking things to heart, and allow the mind to become exhausted because of too much mental pressure of trying to work out what's wrong? This process creates the imbalance or disharmonious situations such as ailments and illness because of our unhappy state. By going within we can reconnect to our infinite power within the heart centre.

Our unhappiness is just a state of mind of thinking we're unhappy, when in fact we have so much to be happy about. So don't allow the negative situations or circumstances within your life to spoil it things us, because we do have a choice, so let's do us a favour, and only embrace the positivity of our learning's because that is our infinite power.

The body as seven main chakra centres, starting with the BASE located at the bottom of the spine which connects us to mother earth. The second is the SACRAL located at the navel and connects us to our gut reactions. The third is the SOLAR PLEXUS located just below the breastbone and connects us to our emotions. The fourth is the HEART located at the heart and connects us to unconditional love. The fifth is the THROAT located at the throat and connects us to direction and expression. The sixth is the BROW located at the brow and connects us to our third eye. The seventh is the CROWN located on top of the head and connects us to the higher conscious self and promotes all knowing.

We then have the higher chakra centres above the crown. The eighth higher MAGENTA chakra connects us to our ascended higher consciousness. The ninth higher SILVER chakra connects us to past lifetimes and our infinite knowledge and wisdom. The tenth higher GOLD chakra connects us to the different levels of enlightenment, and connects us to the creator energy. This level is where miracles can be performed.

The chakra's are like a vortex's that connects you to the universal energy that's around and within the physical body, and is constantly fed throughout by the universal energy. These vortexes energise the body's natural energy system which makes you feel more vibrant and allows you to radiantly shine. The higher chakras above the crown chakra, connects us to the divine, universal energies and the creator, and the base chakra connects us to mother earth.

Around the physical body we have an AURA which is constantly fed by the chakra energy centres; we can also experience blocks or negativity within our aura. The universal energy purifies and cleanses the aura at the same time as the chakras which then purifies and cleanses the physical body on all levels. The aura and chakras are all interconnected, and their relationship maintains a constant flow of energy, free flowing throughout our physical body or mind that interact with our organs, muscles, meridian and acupuncture points, in fact integrates every aspect of us in maintaining our health.

When the energy within our chakras and the different layers of our auras become blocked, our appearance can begin to look dull and we may feel lethargic. When we forget to pay attention to our bodies many needs, we can become ill, often waiting for a medical diagnosis and treatment, before realising that we needed to pay more attention to our bodies in order to maintain well being?

When we treat the cause of our problems or imbalances, we stand more chance of maintaining a well being state that would make a huge difference to every aspect of our lives. When treating any illness, ailment or any disharmonious condition we need to alter our perception about the way we have perceived what's happened to us. We need to treat not just the physical body, but the mind and soul too in order to achieve healing on all levels of our existence, and hopefully prevent any illness, ailments or disease etc from reoccurring.

When we have activated our unique power of self awareness, we become more attuned to the vibrations within and around our physical body and mind. The more body aware we are, will aid us in releasing the imbalances naturally, which allows us to access what we need, in order to enhance our lives. Once this happens, enable us to become mentally, emotionally, physically and spiritually aware at all times.

When we tune into our bodies many needs, it will makes us more aware of the real us, this opens us up to the different techniques we can use in order to release those disharmonious imbalances from within our lives. When we perfect our natural gifts, skills and abilities, would allow us to naturally release the negativity from within our lives, but has the negative situations or circumstances occurs and before they have time to lock into our conscious or sub-conscious minds.

When we understand how our energy system works allows us to release the negativity naturally, and not allowing them to become a major problem before we have to do something about it. Illness and disease can be very time consuming, and it takes all of our efforts and that of others around us in achieving a positive outcome. We must deal with these imbalances before they get out of hand, allowing us to take back the control of our true destiny. We then use our natural gifts, skills and abilities they'll enhance all lives, with us living the life that was intended for us so long ago.

The more evolved we are, the less our physical bodies are effected, allowing us to get a balance between all things within. This allows us to deal with our problems at a much higher vibrational level of consciousness. It is important to understand that whatever we expose ourselves too, there is a Cause and Effect Law! We must all take responsibility for our actions, because if what we do is not about our highest good, and the highest good of all, it will have a negative effect on us with the repercussions affecting all lives.

The mind is powerful, and stores all negative emotions obligingly within the physical body until we have understood the significance of the learning's. Remember this lifetime is about us all having a heavenly life in a human form, and not the one we have created for us out of our unhappiness, and strife.

Our higher consciousness and higher self is the carbon footprint of all that we've ever been, and of whom we are still to become. We are pure energy, and it's important that we reconnect with the infinite energy within, which helps us to maintain a positive attitude to our everyday lives. To be our higher conscious self is to be our true-self, and to see, hear and speak our truth at all times, we must do this in order to achieve a higher conscious state.

Enlightened is who we then become, which allows us to pursue our continued journey of enlightenment. This is our soul's quest, and a journey that we've been on through many lifetimes, searching for the reconnection of our infinite knowledge and wisdom, which is our natural power of divinity.

Depending on our emotional, physical, mental or spiritual issues will denote which category of empowered affirmation would be most beneficial for us. This is why I've designed the different affirmations, putting them into categories for you to work with, eventually leading to the more deep rooted issues within our lives or past lifetimes to reinstate health, wealth and happiness, within every aspect of our lives.

When we understand the energy system within us, we'll realise how we're infinitely connected to the universal energy of creation. But more importantly, how we're all influenced by each other and to what happens within our world. What we read in the newspapers or watch on television has a profound effect on our minds or body's has our hearts reach out to others, in unfortunate situations or circumstances.

We are all affected everyday by things beyond our control, but it's important to realise that we don't have to let ourselves be effected long term. So by just releasing the emotional trauma or upset will allow us to stay calm and collective whilst sending love and healing, to all of those in need.

I have drawn illustrations of the chakra system and aura, so you see how they work separately whilst the universal energy feeds them both in order to purify and cleanse our minds, body and soul completely.

The Chakra system

CHAKRA SYSTEM

side view

UNIVERSAL ENERGY

crown

CROWN —————————————— PURPLE

BROW —————————————— INDIGO

THROAT ————————————— BLUE

HEART ——————————————— GREEN/PINK

SOLAR PLEXUS ————————— YELLOW

SACRAL —————————————— ORANGE

BASE ———————————————— RED

base

EARTHS ENERGY

energy intake

the energy stimulates and purifies the bodies own energy field.

56

The Aura

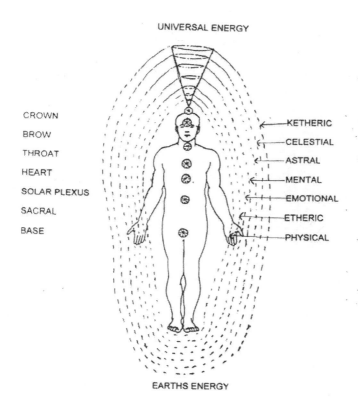

THE SEVEN LAYERS OF THE AURA

UNIVERSAL ENERGY

CROWN

BROW

THROAT

HEART

SOLAR PLEXUS

SACRAL

BASE

KETHERIC

CELESTIAL

ASTRAL

MENTAL

EMOTIONAL

ETHERIC

PHYSICAL

EARTHS ENERGY

layers of the aura in association with the chakra system.

When you are ready and with free will, you can choose to use The Empowered Affirmations Technique, using them has an aid to achieving a Well Being state. The technique is a guideline, and one that has been proven to be successful by myself, and the many clients that have been using this technique or similar techniques over the years.

When you've chosen your empowered affirmation, place your hand over your heart centre, and recite your chosen empowered affirmation in a clear decisive manner. Close your eyes, take a deep breath in, hold and connect with your higher consciousness, the universal energy of the creator, as you breathe out, say out loud I am my infinite power and then allow your mind, body, and soul to rebalance.

Whilst experiencing the affirmations technique you must be standing upright with your feet apart to maintain balance, your feet should have a strong connection to the earth's energy. You will then experience your body rocking or swaying backwards and forwards, and only when you stabilise or have the erg to plunge forwards are you balanced. Remember the rocking sensation can be a gentle swaying to a more forceful sensation, this normally denotes the extent of the imbalance within. If you only swayed gently it's because you were slightly out of balance instead of being totally out of balance. I will go through each process in more detail within the next chapter which allows you to choose your empowered affirmation that best suits your needs!

Now I will explain how the technique works before you use them: We need to re-establish a few personal details before balancing to our true identity and the life that was intended for us.

First, we need to balance to our NAME. This rebalances us to our true-self, and our individual identity of who we really are, which gives us a sense of our place, and right to be, within the structure of all creation.

We then need to rebalance with our ZODIAC sign and with the date & time of our birth (if you know it). This helps to realign us to the astrology charts, solar, and lunar planetary influences of our true nature.

We then need to rebalance with the YIN & YANG in order to balance our feminine and masculine energy in equal measures. This allows us to have a more balanced view of our lives, and to be in perfect harmony with all things within the creation of life.

Then we need to rebalance our CHAKRA'S with us balancing each of our chakras energy systems, starting with the base chakra, and working up towards the crown chakra, and then rebalancing our three higher chakra's which are situated above the crown chakra, and connects us to the creator's infinite energy of our personal and spiritual growth. When balancing each chakra, we must visualise its position within the physical body, and the higher chakras above the physical body, visualising the appropriate colour for each chakra. This allows each chakra to be purified, cleansed, and re-energised, and helps us to feel vibrant and energised, whilst releasing any negative imbalance or emotional issues that we become aware of.

Chakra's within the Body

BASE Chakra   located at the bottom of the spine

SACRAL Chakra   located at the belly button

SOLAR PLEXUS Chakra   located at the stomach

HEART Chakra   located at the heart

THROAT Chakra   located at the throat

BROW Chakra   located on the brow

CROWN Chakra   located at the top of the head

59

Chakra's above the crown and within the Aura

MAGENTA Chakra   2 inches above CROWN Chakra

SILVER Chakra   2 inches above MAGENTA Chakra

GOLD Chakra   2 inches above SILVER Chakra

The universal energy feeds these chakras constantly but when our chakras become blocked with negative energy, these chakras can't function properly, so they become depleted, which leaves us with low energy. If these blocked chakras are left untreated they would cause us to feel lethargic or to suffer from fatigued, illness or disease. This would then have an adverse affect our physical bodies with us feeling unwell or depressed. It's important that we maintain a constant flow of positive energy pulsating throughout our entire bodies, re-energising and purifying the mind, body and soul. So by drawing an empowered affirmation that seems appropriate to our feelings or issues will help to eradicate disharmonious situations.

We need to rebalance to our HIGHER CONSCIOUS self, which will allow us to analyze our negative issues, again just let yourself be drawn to the affirmation that best suits your needs, eventually reciting all of the empowered affirmations for this category. This aids in our spiritual and personal growth, empowering the mind and body to reconnect with our soul. It important to be reunited with our inner-self, inner-being and essential self. We also need to reconnect with our intuition at a higher conscious state. The higher conscious affirmations can empower us to become our truth, and connect with our infinite power once more.

We need to rebalance to the different aspects of our LIFE allowing us to analyze our problems or issues within our everyday lives. We have to recognise where we are being blocked and too why? Maybe it's because of some fear or limiting belief that's stopping us from moving forwards. So just let yourself be drawn to an affirmation that best suits your needs, allowing yourself to be honest with yourself as to what is really wrong within your life.

We need to rebalance to the true meaning of LOVE allowing us to analyze our problems then we can take action by choosing an affirmation that feels most appropriate to our needs or particular problem. Empower yourself to allow the universe to deliver a great love to you or to reignite passion within an existing relationship or even self love. We have to love ourselves before can truly love another, and also we need to love us with all our imperfections, and be accepting of all things.

We need to rebalance to PROSPERITY allowing us to analyze our problems as to why you feel blocked to prosperity. Allow yourself to choose an affirmation that will empower you. Maybe you do not feel deserving in some way? Or you're not open to receiving or to the law of attraction. To attract prosperity we need to be at one with ourselves and in the present moment, in order to manifest all that we need to live abundantly within our chosen lifestyle.

We need to rebalance to the SUPPORT SYSTEM of the universe, which allows us to analyze our problems of why we feel unsupported in life. We must try to understand what sorts of support we need, and make sure we're open, and accepting of that support. At times we refuse the support that's offered because we suddenly realise we don't need help for whatever reason! So when you are ready, allow yourself to choose an affirmation that best suits your needs or compose one for yourself that offers a more complete solution, because we're all unique, and individual in every-way. It's important that we are honest with ourselves to our needs with us trusting in the outcome when reciting an affirmation.

We need to rebalance to the different aspects or circumstances of our PAST LIFETIMES which will allow us to address our present day issues, by letting go of any past

61

lifetime influences that are no longer relevant to this life. We have to ask us why we keep repeating the same old patterns, programs, and the same old mistakes over, and over again. We all have past life issues to overcome, as they're part and parcel of our life's path and purpose or lessons, and when we've fully understood, and overcome these lessons they will allow us to follow our true path and destiny, through life.

This process will ultimately allow us to take back control of our everyday lives, and give us great understanding of our truth, and of whom we really are. Releasing past lifetime issues will set us free to become a powerful being once more and allows us access to our limitless potential. We can empower us to achieve anything we want, we've all being successful in other lifetimes, achieving health, wealth, and happiness.

You can also realign us to the MIND, BODY AND SOUL energies, by reciting an empowered affirmation. When reciting the affirmation imagine a triangle pointing upwards to connect you to the mind, body and soul. This will realign you with the different elements, and structure for your earthly life.

You can also realign to the UNIVERSAL, COSMIC, AND EARTH energies by reciting an empowered affirmation. When reciting the affirmation imagine a triangle pointing downwards to connect you to the universe, cosmic and earth's energies. This realigns you with the whole of creation, and your earthly life.

When we have successfully worked through the exercise of balancing our energy field and releasing the negative blocks from within, we should feel really good about ourselves. We will notice a big difference in how we feel, more alert and alive, and positive about our futures. We will worry less, and take things more in our strides, knowing that there is plenty of time to achieve our dreams, accepting that it is all happening in divine timing.

When we need to re-balance our energy system just allow yourself to feel where you are out of balance? So stand with your feet apart with your feet connected to mother earth, next hold your head up high and connect with the universe. Then allow yourself to relax, close your eyes and hold your hand over the heart centre, and just sense your energy, do you feel balanced? Does the Yin and Yang energy feel balanced or does one side feel heavier than the other? Do any of the Chakras feel unbalanced? If so, just set about re-balancing your energy system, the more you re-balance your energy the more body-aware you become.

Get a worksheet: And write down any problems or issues, ailments or illness that you want to work with. Try to understand the emotional undertone to any problem or imbalance that you have, and allow yourself to work out what is really going on within you. It is about being truthful with yourself, and to what you really want from your life! So ask yourself question like!

Why do I feel blocked?

Why do I keep making the same mistakes over and over again?

Why can I not achieve my dreams or ambitions?

Why do I feel disheartened or unhappy?

Why do I feel out of balance and unwell?

Why do I expect failure?

Why am I procrastinating?

Why am I justifying my actions?

Why am I attracting negativity?

Why am I blaming others or the different situations for what is wrong within my life?

Why am I living in the past or future when I should be living in the Now!

Why am I not taking responsibility for myself or my actions?

Why am I not achieving my full potential?

Why am I holding onto resentment, regrets or anger?

Why is my life such a struggle?

Why don't I love myself or even like myself?

Why don't I have faith, belief or trust in me anymore?

Why don't I trust my decisions and act upon them?

Why do I feel insecure?

Why do I give my power away to others by focusing on them, when my need is greater?

Why have I lost my confidence?

Why do I feel a victim of my own doing?

Why have I given up on my life, because all I do is just go through the motions?

Why do I blame myself for things that are not my fault?

Why do I feel hard done too?

Why do I feel like I'm being punished for a crime I haven't committed?

Why do I take advice as criticism?

Why do I push others to succeed when I can't?

Why do I let my fears stop me from achieving?

Why am I feeling depressed or down?

Why do I feel despondency or gloom?

The above quotes are just a guideline to help us seek and speak our truth to how we are really feeling. When we are honest with us, we can then solve the problems or issues within our lives instantly.

The power of affirmations has a profound effect on the mind, body and soul. They allow us to reprogram old thought patterns and beliefs, altering our perceptions about the different situations and circumstances within our lives. When we empower us the new thought program will have an adverse effect on how the mind then influences the physical body, which alters our state of consciousness, and well being state. When reciting positive affirmations and with the reconnection to the life-force energy, our physical bodies and minds, respond positively.

This process re-educate us to become more self and body-aware, and allows us to listen to our bodies many needs, and enables us to re-address any life's experience or issues that leave us feeling emotionally or mentally drained? If we do not address these issues we take the risk of creating disharmonious situations within that can disrupt our lives, by us being ill or feeling depressed, and blocked within our lives.

It is important that we take responsibility for us, and our well being state. We owe it to us to maintain health on all levels, reenergising and revitalising our energy system. All that we need is within to maintain health, but if we just concentrate in an external way to achieve a well being state, we end up giving our power away or we dilute its potential by not recognising it's within, and makes us a powerful human being.

We need conventional medicine, and at times surgery in order to achieve a healthy body, but we must also play a personal part in maintaining health by altering our perception to the different situations or circumstances that's happened to us, and within our lives. We need to release the imbalances from within our minds, body and soul, and allow us to achieve healing that will make us feel whole and complete once more.

By being more accepting of life's trials and tribulations, and to address those disharmonious issues, we can then influence the mind that in turn influences the body into achieving well being state. It really is mind over matter, and we have a responsibility to us to ensure a healthy and happy; life for us.

We hold the power to rejuvenate, invigorate and heal the psychic body, mind and soul. We have been unable to heal our bodies properly because we'd disconnected from the power within that would perform the miracles we need, often from a lack of faith, belief and trust in us. We pay too much time and attention on perfecting an outer show of achieving, sometimes pushing ourselves to the absolute limits, not realising how hard we've been on us, until we become ill. This results in the unrest of our soul or inner-self, with us still striving for the next quick fix that makes us feel good about ourselves and lives, while we persist in masking the unrest or disharmonious feelings within.

So now I've explained how the technique works? We start with us re-establishing our physical-self to our inner true self, with the acceptance of our higher conscious self has being a natural part of us. With us re-establishing our earthly identity of whom we really are, and is important to our continued growth on all levels of existence. With the reestablishment of this unique power creates an infinite supply of energy that maintains well being on all levels, and will serve us well until the end of time.

THE EMPOWERED AFFIRMATIONS

So let's begin... Start by writing the affirmation that you're going to recite onto a card in order to hold in front of you or recite straight from the book whilst you experience the empowered affirmations technique. When we honour and respect ourselves, we can empower us with the creator divine infinite energy, evoking our true power of conviction, intention focus, and direction.

We start with empowering us to our higher consciousness' definition of the key elements of our perception of truth. We do this in order to make us empowered with the transition of our lower conscious self, to our higher conscious self, and reconnect to the truth of all aspects of us that will allows us to feel fulfilment and contentment in all that we do. To change our perception or the way we feel about our lives takes commitment and dedication. We must empower us to be responsible for all aspects of us and alleviating our imbalances from within our everyday lives. The empowered affirmations technique will allow you to embrace your higher consciousness where a profound healing takes place on all levels of our existence.

NAME AFFIRMATION

So let's start by empowering the self with our full name, we do this because we must be accepting of us completely. So when you're ready, stand up straight with feet apart for balance, and connect to the earth's energy. Place your hand or project your minds energy to the heart centre, and recite the empowered affirmation listed below in a clear decisive manner stating your full name, then close your eyes, and take a deep breath in and hold, then connect with your higher consciousness and universal energy of the creator, and allow your minds energy to expand upwards. As you breathe out, say I am my infinite power and allow yourself to rebalance to your name.

The Empowered Name Affirmation:

I am unique in everyway and I honour and respect myself. I rejoice in my name of, stating your full name ....

ZODIAC AFFIRMATION

To empower yourself with your zodiac sign and date of birth, stand up straight with feet apart for balance, and connect to the earth's energy. Place your hand over the heart, and recite the empowered affirmation listed below in a clear decisive manner stating your zodiac details, then close your eyes, take a deep breath in, hold, and connect with your higher consciousness, and universal energy of the creator, and allow your minds energy to expand upwards. As you breathe out, say I am my infinite power and allow yourself to rebalance to your zodiac sign.

The Empowered Zodiac Affirmation:

I interconnect with all planetary, lunar and solar systems. They are all encompassing with the universe, the earth's elements and rhythmic cycles. I am at one with myself and the whole of creation and my zodiac sign of? And then state your date of birth and the time you were born if you know it!

YIN & YANG AFFIRMATION

It is important to balance your yin and yang, the feminine and masculine energy. Stand up straight with feet apart for balance, and connect to the earth's energy. Place your hand or project your minds energy to the heart centre, recite the empowered affirmation listed below in a clear decisive manner, close your eyes, take a deep breath in and hold, and connect with your higher consciousness, and universal energy of the creator, and allow your minds energy to expand upwards. As you breathe out, say I am my infinite power and allow yourself to rebalance to your Yin & Yang.

The Empowered Yin & Yang Affirmation:

I balance my feminine and masculine energy in perfect harmony. My yin and yang are in equal measures and they support me at all times. They make me feel whole and complete, and I am balanced at all times which makes me a powerful being.

CHAKRA AFFIRMATIONS

There are seven main chakras within the body and three higher chakras which are located above the crown chakra. When you have balanced all ten of your chakras you will then be reconnected to your higher consciousness of the universe, cosmic realms and the creator. Stand up straight with feet apart for balance, and connect to the earth's energy. Place your hand or project your minds energy to the heart centre, and recite the empowered affirmation listed below in a clear decisive manner that's related to the chakra you are rebalancing, starting with the Base. Visualise the colour associated with the chakra, close your eyes, take a deep breath in and hold connect with your higher consciousness, and universal energy of the creator, and allow your minds energy to expand upwards. As you breathe out, say I am my infinite power and rebalance to the energy of the chakra that you are working with.

Remember to start at the base chakra and work upwards to the crown chakra, then the three higher chakras above the crown. You can make a list of the chakras and write down which chakra was out of balance and to what extent.

The Empowered Chakra Affirmations

BASE CHAKRA = RED

I accept my birthright, and I am grounded, safe and secure at all times. I have faith, belief and trust in my true-self and the process of my life's purpose.

SACRAL CHAKRA = ORANGE

I have conviction of my truth and I trust in my higher conscious self. I initiate my creativity in all that I do, and I am centred and balanced.

SOLAR PLEXUS CHAKRA =YELLOW

I have quality in certainty in all I think, say or do. I am vibrant and joyous, and with self worth and belief in myself, my future is safe and secure.

HEART CHAKRA = GREEN/PINK

I love myself unconditionally and I have dedication and self realisation. I am open to giving and receiving. I love and accept myself and others completely.

THROAT CHAKRA = BLUE

I ask for what I want with truth, conviction and expression. I can manifest my dreams and ambitions, and I realise my potential now.

BROW CHAKRA = INDIGO

I trust in my life and all experiences, and I act on my intuition and insight to lead the way confidently, joyfully and in truth.

CROWN CHAKRA = PURPLE

My spiritual being interpenetrates and creates everything out of its own infinite energy. I am connected to universal love, the infinite knowledge wisdom, at all times.

HIGHER CHAKRA = MAGENTA

I ignite my higher heart embers into a magenta flame, opening the gateway to my higher consciousness and self, which fills me with joy and blissfulness.

HIGHER CHAKRA = SILVER

I ignite the star fire from the scared flame, and I arise stronger from the ashes of my old self into my new self, in all my magnificence and glory.

HIGHER CHAKRA = GOLD

I have ascended to my higher consciousness which connects me to the cosmic and universal realms of unity. The mystical gateway as now opened to me, and I am totally supported by the universe and bask in unconditional love.

The chakras can from time to time get clogged with negative energy, so it's important to rebalance them once you recognise that the energy within a chakra feels depleted in some way. The more that you re-balance these important centres the more you become self and body aware, and the stronger the connection to the infinite energy. This will have a positive effect on your aura where you will physically begin to look and feel more vibrant and radiant.

Keeping a record of the chakra's that you felt were blocked or out of balance will act as a reminder to rebalance your chakra's on a regular basis, because as you remove the negativity from within our chakra's and physical body, our energy will change and vibrate more refined. The chakra system and the layers of the aura, interact, all working together in maintaining a well being state, bringing balance and harmony to your mind, body and soul, once more.

The purification and cleansing process of the chakra's and aura will enhance health, allowing you to feel and look younger, and more vibrant. This gives you more energy and the ability to pursue your dreams and goals through to completion. When our chakra's are rebalanced they make us more accepting of all situations or circumstances which allow us to go with the flow of life.

HEAL MY LIFE AFFIRMATIONS

Just allow yourself to be drawn to an empowered affirmations listed below, eventually doing them all if you wish. Stand up straight with feet apart for balance, and connect to the earth's energy. Place your hand or project your minds energy to your heart centre, and recite your chosen affirmation in a clear decisive manner and close your eyes, take a deep breath in and hold, connect with your higher consciousness, and universal energy of the creator, and allow your minds energy to expand upwards. As you breathe out, say I am my infinite power and rebalance to your life.

The Empowered Heal my Life Affirmations:

I am part of the rhythm of life, and I flow with divine energy in order to heal the different imbalances within my life.

I am totally at one with all of life, and the universe supports me continuously.

All is well within my life and I release all negativity that no longer serves a purpose.

I create a life filled with love, joy and laughter. My life is full of love, and I am healthy and wise.

Life loves me and I love my life, and I live my life to the full.

I go beyond my fears and limitations, and create the life I want.

All that I ask for is with love and joy in my heart and soul.

I am centred and peaceful, and it's safe for me to be alive and well, achieving well being.

I am my infinite power, and I have integrity and truth in my world. I am at peace and I'm happy.

I am filled with confidence, love and infinite energy, and I enjoy blissful living always.

I flow freely with new experiences and directions. I allow my life to move on and situations to change.

It is my birthright to be fully in my life. I am totally supported by the earth and universal energies.

I am at one with myself, and with the family of life. I love my life and live it just for me.

I am at peace and comfortable with every stage of my life. I am happy, confident, safe and secure.

I recognise my full potential and it's safe for me to be fully in my life right now

I am connected to my dreams and visions, and I can manifest them successfully now.

I am in perfect balance and harmony. I move forwards in my life with ease at every stage.

The life force energy naturally flows through me and around me at all times, keeping me healthy.

I release all restrictions and restraints within my life to the universe. All is peaceful, and I'm safe and secure.

All aspects of my life work together in perfect harmony. I dance to the joyous rhythm of universal energy which sets me free.

I move beyond my limitations, and I am universally supported and guided at all times.

I take in life in perfect balance and with joy and ease.

I go with the flow of life confidently and happily.

I am united and balanced with all aspects of my life. I love my life.

I accept my full power as a (say your gender) man or women and I accept all my bodily processes as normal and natural. I am healthy and happy.

I relax into the flow of life and I let life provide all that I need. I show gratitude for all I have within my life now and for what's still to come.

I experience life as a joyous dance with joy in my heart and soul.

I open my heart and create only a loving relationship with all aspects of my life.

I only attract loving relationships.

My life is joyful and full of love and laughter.

I embrace all that I have now become and to whom I am still to be.

I realise and achieve my full potential, and it's safe for me to be fully in my life right now.

I am totally supported by the universe.

All that I need comes to me and I'm safe and secure with the knowledge that my potential is limitless.

My life is rich with love and happiness.

I choose this life for its experiences, and my lessons have set me free.

I now choose to live my life in perfect harmony.

I know how to be healthy of mind, body and soul.

I know how to process life's experiences so it doesn't take its toll on my mind or body.

I heal my life by releasing anger, resentment or hurt from within.

I heal my life by releasing ailments or illness from within.

(In fact you can release any negative imbalance or condition from within) Just by saying I heal my life stating the condition or aliment, and then release the negativity within.

LOVE AFFIRMATIONS

Just allow yourself to be drawn to an affirmation off the empowered affirmations listed below. Stand up straight with feet apart for balance and connect to the earth's energy. Place your hand or project your minds energy to the heart centre, and recite your chosen affirmation in a clear decisive manner, close your eyes and take a deep breath in and hold, connect with your higher consciousness, and the universal energy of the creator, and allow your minds energy to expand upwards. As you breathe out, say I am my infinite power and rebalance to your love energy, self love and unconditional love.

The Empowered Love Affirmations:

I love myself totally and with all my imperfections; all is well within my life.

It is safe to be me and to be my truth at all times. I accept and love myself.

75

I love and approve of myself, and I realise my self-worth and potential.

My inner being loves it's self.

I love and approve of myself, I am loving and lovable.

I accept all that I have within my life, has it's all a part of my life's path and purpose.

I lovingly take care and nourish my mind, body and soul.

I love and rejoice in each cycle and at each stage of my life.

I forgive myself totally for my wrongs, and rejoice in the power of me and my truth.

I rejoice in who I am. I am a beautiful expression of life.

I am love and I now see others with love unconditionally.

I give myself permission to move forwards with my life, and I love my life.

I am love and know the universe always supports me when I go with the flow of life effortlessly.

My heart beats to the rhythm of love, and I allow the universe to deliver a great love to me now.

I am love and I see all things with love. Love is within my heart and soul, now and forever.

I forgive myself and all situations. I am now free to love me and others unconditionally.

Our creator please forgive me because I cannot forgive myself, and thus I will be released from my sins.

I forgive myself for all my just deeds and others for theirs.

I am pure love, and unconditional love flows through me now and forever.

I am totally supported by the universal love and I bask in all its glory.

I only see with love and clarity, and I have a clear vision of my future.

I love myself enough to say no to the demands of others.

I am the most important person in my life. I love me and I am my truth and true-self at all times.

I honour and respect myself completely.

My femininity nurtures me and guides me with intuitive principles. I am connected to all things.

My masculinity nurtures me and guides me with codes of ethics and conduct. I am equal to all things.

I heal my sexuality and enjoy being feminine. I have joy in my heart and soul at all times (ladies only)

I heal my sexuality and enjoy being masculine. I have joy in my heart and soul at all times. (Men only)

I rejoice in all relationships including my relationship with me. I am free to be me in all that I do.

I am tolerant and kind to me and others at all times.

I love myself unconditionally and I open myself up to receiving even more love.

I allow myself to receive a relationship of true love, and on a soul connection. Please deliver that love to me now.

SUPPORT AFFIRMATIONS

Just allow yourself to be drawn to an affirmation off the empowered affirmations listed below. Stand up straight with feet apart for balance, and connect to the earth's energy. Place your hand or project your minds energy to the heart centre, and then recite the chosen affirmation in a clear decisive manner, close your eyes, take a deep breath in and hold, and connect with your higher consciousness, and the universal energy of the creator, and allow your minds energy to expand upwards. As you breathe out, say I am my infinite power and rebalance to your own support system.

The Empowered Support Affirmations:

My thinking is peaceful, calm and centred. In acceptance I am my own power.

I have a right to be here, and I rejoice in my position in life.

I feel love, peace and compassion for all people, myself included at all times.

There are harmonious solutions to the problems that I find myself in, and I accept them right now.

I joyfully move on to experience new levels of existence of my life's journey and quest of my soul.

I lovingly take back my power of divinity and eliminate all interference now.

It is my birthright to have all my needs met. I now ask for what I want with love and truth.

I move into my greater good. My good is everywhere and I am safe and secure. All is well.

I declare peace and harmony indwell within me and surround me at all times.

I support myself completely and wholeheartedly.

My loving thoughts and actions keep my immune system strong. All is well and balanced.

Every experience is perfect for my growth process. I am at peace now.

II release the conditions or situations in my consciousness that has created my problems. I am willing to change by releasing them and setting myself free.

I trust in my inner voice. I am strong, wise and powerful, and I hear my truth at all times.

I am connected to the family of life, and I'm totally supported by everyone.

It is safe to see the viewpoints of others as well as my own. We all contribute to the bigger picture of life.

I have faith in myself. I am connected with my higher self and consciousness.

I have belief in myself. I am connected to the belief I will succeed in all I do.

I have trust in myself. I am connected with my higher consciousness' definition of trust.

I am connected to my higher consciousness' definition of truth of all things.

I forgive myself, others, and all situations that have not been about the highest good of all.

I connect to the earth's structure and the universe, which gives me a firm foundation on which to build the rest of my life upon.

I no longer beat myself up for things I feel I have got wrong. For they are a part of my life's purpose and learning's.

I am comfortable with my sexuality and I rejoice in my own expression. I am my creative power.

I am willing to forgive the past and rejoice in my infinite knowledge and wisdom, and go beyond my limitations now.

I take full responsibility for all of my needs, and I nourish and respect myself at all times.

I only send out loving thoughts, and only loving thoughts come back to me.

All I do is in truth. Truth is what I seek, and truth is what I attract at all times.

It is safe for me to move forwards with my life. I now let go of the restraints and restrictions from within my life.

I move forwards in my life and it's safe to let go of all my burdens for they no longer serve a purpose.

I no longer need to protect myself so I release all negativity associated with being overweight.

I am a beautiful expression of my true-self, and I love myself completely.

If you have an addiction that you are trying to overcome you can use the affirmation below and fill in the gap with your addiction, for example Drugs, Alcohol, Cigarettes, Chocolate etc!

I no longer need to .... anymore. I release all negativity associated with my addiction. I now take back control of myself and my life, and I will nourish and respect my mind, body and soul at all times.

PAST LIFETIMES AFFIRMATIONS

Just allow yourself to be drawn to an affirmation off the empowered affirmations listed below. Stand up straight with feet apart for balance and connect to the earth's energy. Place your hand or project your minds energy to your heart centre, and then recite your chosen affirmation in a clear decisive manner, close your eyes, take a deep breath in, hold and connect with your higher consciousness, and the universal energy of the creator, and allow your minds energy to expand upwards. As you breathe out, say I am my infinite power and then rebalance to your past lifetimes energy, connecting with your limitless potential of all lives.

The Empowered Past Lifetimes Affirmations:

It is with love that I totally release the past. I am safe and all is well within my life.

The past is released and I choose to live in the now.

I love and respect myself and trust in the process of this life. I am safe and secure.

I release the restraints and restrictions of the past and move forwards with love and joy in my heart and soul.

I comfortably and easily release the old and welcome the new within my life. I flow with the eternal life force energy.

I joyously release my fears and I am safe and secure.

I am willing to forgive the past and rejoice in my infinite knowledge and wisdom. It's safe for me to go beyond my limitations now.

I release all negativity from my past lifetimes or this life, on the deeper fundamental levels of my being.

My past life has served a deeper purpose and I release all negative emotions associated with that life. I am safe and well.

My past and present are now one. I am the interpretation of my infinite soul.

I free myself from my negative emotions of the past that has affected my life, mind, body or soul. I am now free.

I release and conditions, ailments or illness associated with the past. I am free to be healthy of mind, body and soul and I achieve a well being state.

I release Disease that has affected my mind, body or soul. Miracles do happen, everyday in everyway and I accept a healing miracle right now.

I allow the positive attributes from all lifetimes to be bestowed upon me now, and I will use them to the highest good of all.

I release the past and allow time to heal every aspect of my life.

I rejoice and show gratitude of my life's experiences and their learning's have set me free from my own insecurities.

I live in the now and my future is bright, and I'm safe and well.

I release the fears associated with what I want to accomplish right now. I will succeed and be successful in all I do.

I release my fear that's deep rooted and associated with my life's purpose and learning's.

With love in my heart and soul no harm will ever come to me. I am safe and protected at all times.

My knowledge and wisdom is a true record of my infinite soul's achievements of all lifetimes.

I am a limitless being.

My past, present and future are merging into one and I will achieve my limitless potential, and become successful in all I do in the Now.

PROSPERITY AFFIRMATIONS

Just allow yourself to be drawn to an affirmation off the empowered affirmations listed below. Stand up straight with feet apart for balance, and connect to the earth's energy. Place your hand or project your minds energy to the heart centre, and then recite your chosen affirmation in a clear decisive manner, close your eyes, and take a deep breath in and hold, connect with your higher consciousness, and universal energy of the creator, and allow your minds energy to expand upwards. As you breathe out, say I am my infinite power and rebalance to your prosperity energy.

The Empowered Prosperity Affirmations:

I give myself permission to be the best I can be.

I recognise my unique gifts, skills, talents and abilities, and I use them now to the highest good of all, and achieving my limitless potential.

I now choose to create a life that is joyous and filled with abundance. All is well within my life now, and I am prosperous in all I do.

I am motivated, enthusiastic and passionate about life. Life is for me, and prosperity is my true destiny.

I have the strength, power and skills to attract all that I need from life. I promise to fulfil my dreams and ambitions now.

I am my creative power, and I fully appreciate my life and all that I have.

I attract the power of money, I am successful and confident, and I am my infinite power.

I recognise the opportunities within my life, they are the small steps to becoming successful and fulfilling my dreams and goals.

I am my creativity and choose to express myself in all that I do, think or say. I am a true expression of life and attract what I need positively.

I have courage and conviction, and I believe in myself to achieve all that I want.

I am in perfect harmony with the universe; my actions are aligned with the highest good of all.

Self observation and self knowledge is essential to self growth and success.

In accordance of my life, my duties have been prescribed for me and as I follow them, my desires and ambitions will naturally be fulfilled.

With self-effort and my pre-destiny they become my power for success, and help me achieve my potential in all that I desire.

My positive thoughts and actions give me the opportunity to succeed and be successful.

I go with the flow of life; allowing me to be accepting of all things, and to recognise when it's the right time for action in order to succeed.

I will not allow myself to feel threatened by the decisions or choices of others; I am safe and secure at all times.

I have the ability to recognise my worth, and give myself permission to go beyond my limitations. I will succeed.

I have the faith and patience to allow everything to unfold naturally in divine and universal timing.

I attract abundance and I can manifest my dreams and desires now with conviction.

I attract all that I need in a positive and rewarding way.

I embrace all opportunities and challenges in my life, for they give me the chance to achieve my dreams.

I give myself permission to go beyond my wildest dreams now.

I dare to dare, and I will win and succeed. I am confident and I'm now ready to move forwards with my life.

I embrace my gifts, skills and abilities, and I am my creative power, expressing my true-self within my creativity.

I am my infinite power and I am connected to my full potential, and I will succeed in all that I do.

I give myself the permission to seek the truth of all things, and to show compassion and understanding to myself and others.

I am non-judgemental, and I promise to be tolerant and kind to others who are less fortunate than me.

Prosperity is my true destiny and the true destiny of all, and there is more than enough for us all to share.

I live my life just for me so I can prosper in all that I do. My life is already so rewarding and fun as I share what I have with everyone.

Prosperity comes in many ways and forms, I show gratitude for all that I already have, and for the prosperity that I am still to receive. Thank You!

THE HIGHER CONSCIOUS AFFIRMATIONS

Just allow yourself to be drawn to an affirmation from the empowered affirmations listed below, eventually doing all of them if you wish. Choose an Empowered Affirmations that you feel drawn too. Stand up straight with feet apart for balance, and connect to the earth's energy. Place your hand or project your minds energy to the heart centre, and then recite your chosen affirmation in a clear decisive manner. Close your eyes, and take a deep breath in and hold, connect with your higher consciousness and universal energy of the creator and allow your minds energy to expand upwards. As you breathe out, say I am my infinite power and rebalance to your higher conscious self.

The Empowered Higher Conscious Affirmations:

I am my higher conscious self, my truth and I embrace my limitless potential.

I am connected to my divine nature, and innate knowledge and wisdom.

I connected to unconditional love, the universe and the cosmic' infinite energy and they support me at all times.

I draw love, strength and inspiration from the divine, the universe and the cosmic realms.

I am totally supported by the universal energy that sustains all life, and all that I need comes to me.

I am my higher consciousness, and my infinite knowledge and wisdom makes me powerful.

In truth, acceptance and integrity, I am my higher conscious power and I manifest all that I need in divine timing.

I rejoice in my true self and my higher conscious self completely.

In pure consciousness I have poise, tranquillity and peace. I am whole and complete once more.

I allow myself to receive divine inspiration and guidance. This will increase my psychic and intuitive powers and abilities at all times.

I am a divine channel for the universe to bestow its spiritual and psychic abundance upon me now.

My soul's journey to enlightenment is ongoing and eternal. I am my infinite power at all times and I rejoice in all my accomplishments and achievements.

I show gratitude and acknowledge my place within the cosmic order of life, and give thanks for all that I have and for all that's still to come.

I realise my potential which allows me to be my higher conscious self and truth at all times.

My higher consciousness releases me from the restraints and restrictions of my lower conscious self.

My higher consciousness is my truth and I am dedicated to seeking my truth at all times.

My higher conscious self is my inner hearing, inner seeing and intuitive knowing at all times.

My higher consciousness allows me to be the best I can be, and to achieve all that I desire consciously.

My higher conscious self and my lower conscious self work in perfect harmony. I am my true power, and I will be successful in all that I do.

I am my higher consciousness and I walk the pathway of my true destiny.

With my higher consciousness I am my infinite power which empowers me, and allows me to be free from all of my restraints and restrictions.

I allow my negative blocks associated with my clairvoyance to dissolve and disappear. I am worthy of my unique gifts. I am open to my abilities of clairvoyance seeing with love, light and truth.

I allow any negative blocks associated with my clairaudience to dissolve and disappear. I am worthy of this unique gift and I am open to clairaudience now. I hear with love and truth in my heart and soul.

I allow my negative blocks associated with my clairsentience to dissolve and disappear. I am worthy of this unique gift and I am open to my clairsentience now. I will listen to my inner guidance at all times.

I will speak my truth and hear my truth at all times. I am my higher consciousness and my higher self, in love, light and truth.

I honour my higher conscious self as I tread the pathway to my ascended self now, with integrity, honour and pure intention.

MIND, BODY & SOUL AFFIRMATION

When you feel you have sorted out your negative issues, you can achieve realignment with the Mind, Body & Soul. This will ground you into the structure of the earth giving you a strong foundation for physical, mental and spiritual growth and will connect you to your soul and the universe. Stand up straight with your feet apart for balance, and connect to the earth's energy. Place your hand or project your minds energy to the heart centre, and visualise the Mind, Body, & Soul triangle, then recite the affirmation listed below in a clear decisive manner, close your eyes, take a deep breath in, hold and connect with your higher consciousness, universal energy of the creator and allow your minds energy to expand upwards. As you breathe out, say I am my infinite power and rebalance to the realignment of your mind, body and soul.

The Empowered Mind, Body & Soul Affirmation.

With my mind, body and soul I honour my place on earth. All that I do will be to the highest good of all, and in truth, light and love.

The triangle represents the mind, body & soul.

SOUL

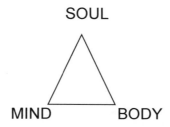

MIND   BODY

EARTH, UNIVERSE & COSMIC AFFIRMATION

When you are ready you can now do the one for the Earth, Universe and Cosmic realignment. This will connect you to the earth, universe, and the cosmic realms and beyond, giving you a strong connection to your higher consciousness, infinite knowledge and wisdom, and truth. Stand up straight with your feet apart for balance, and connect to the earth's energy. Place your hand or project you minds energy to the heart centre, and visualize the Earth, Universe, & Cosmic triangle, then recite the affirmation listed below in a clear decisive manner, close your eyes, take a deep breath in, hold and connect with your higher consciousness, universal energy of the creator, and allow your minds energy to expand upwards. As you breathe out, say I am my infinite power and rebalance to the realignment of the earth, universe and cosmic realms.

The Empowered Earth, Universe & Cosmic Affirmation:

With my mind, body and soul, I honour my place on earth with connection to the earth, universe and cosmic realms. All that I do will be to the highest good of humankind. I am now whole and complete, and my truth once more.

The triangle represents the earth, universe & cosmic.

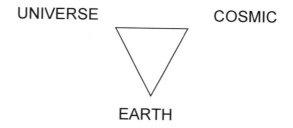

When you have completed all the affirmations above, feel free to re-empower yourself at anytime. If you feel that you need to do any one of the affirmations again, you can! If you plunge forwards straight away the definition of the empowered affirmation is still intact. If not, then there is an understanding still to be achieved. Remember you can compose any of the affirmations to suit your requirements or you can make up your own as long as they are a clear decisive statement, the power is in the words and the conviction in which they are recited.

To empower yourself is to let go of old thoughts and programming, and to re-educate yourself with a new thought process, and by changing your perception to the different situations or circumstances that still affect you. The way we allow the different negative issues to affect us, will denote how our body, mind or soul responds to any situation that we find ourselves in. The process of empowerment has a profound effect upon our well being states, it's important that we don't let ourselves be compromised by our insecurities or fears. So hypothetically what's happened to us we have allowed to happen, and we can change our perception anytime we like by turning any negative situation into a positive learning.

We can COMMAND what we want from life but we have to send the positive command to the brain first. By doing this we can activate an extraordinary degree of power from speaking to the super conscious mind. The empowered affirmations counteract negative beliefs or programming which gives us back control of our everyday lives. With the highly targeted commands we can transform our minds and body's almost instantaneously which allows us to attract what we need straight away.

With positive thoughts and actions we can achieve our limitless potential by attracting what we need by reciting a positive, realistic, COMMAND to the universe and our higher consciousness. Magically you will be able to manifest all your dreams and desires, it's no big secret to achieving success, all you have to do is re-connect with your infinite power that's within. Empowering yourself with your higher consciousness and ascended self, this is your true vocation in its truest form.

The two triangles also represent the blade and the chalice, the masculine and feminine energy. What's above is below and the duality of all aspects of life as we know it.

BLADE   CHALICE

When we place the two triangles over each other they form The Star of David.

SOUL

UNIVERSE   COSMIC

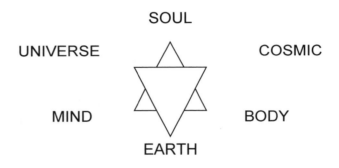

MIND   BODY

EARTH

THE STAR OF CREATION

The Star of Creation is also known as The Star of David, and is often used as a talisman with the interpretation left to each individual or organisation to decipher. The Star symbolizes our infinite power, the unity of humankind and all of creation.

The six-pointed star is of ancient origin, and used in many religions with a variety of meanings. There meanings explicit the power of the symbol, and it's been used for occult and ceremonial magic. It also represents the wonders of our world and all of creation, with the interpretation of life's experiences and events.

The illustration shows that when you place the two triangles over each other, creates a star which illustrates the realignment of the mind, body and soul, to the earth, universe and cosmic vibrations. This allows the realignment of the lower conscious self, to the higher conscious self, which creates an oneness within, and allows us to feel whole and complete as we embark on the next part of our soul's journey of ascension.

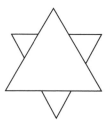

The Star of Creation represents our power within, and symbolizes Power, Wisdom, Majesty, Love, Mercy, and Justice. When we balance the energy of our mind, body and soul with the earth, universe, and cosmic energy, will allow us access to the collective consciousness of us, humankind and our creator. This is our unique power within, and once we've embraced that power, we can fulfil our obligation and commitment to living our lives, to the best of our abilities.

Our perception of life's experiences denotes our level of consciousness and truth, at any given time. The truth cannot be argued with, and our justifications are not our truth!

The truth is the power that will set us free; to become all knowing, is to be at one with us. When we're at one with us, we'll instinctively know what the truth is of any given situation or circumstance. Our truth is not necessarily someone else's truth, because we're all on our own individual paths of seeking the truth of our soul's quest and purpose.

The two triangles of the Star of David also represent our conscious and sub-conscious minds. The triangle pointing upwards represents our conscious mind, and denotes our higher conscious us and journey of ascension. The triangle pointing downwards represents our sub-conscious mind, and denotes our lower conscious us and earthly existence.

The Star of Creation represents all things encompassing, self-love, belief, faith and trust in us, is a powerful combination and important to our well being. This is our infinite power within, and aids us in achieving success in all that we do.

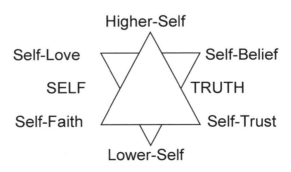

CONSCIOUS MIND

Higher-Self

Self-Love   Self-Belief

SELF   TRUTH

Self-Faith   Self-Trust

Lower-Self

SUB-CONSCIOUS MIND

When we are true to us, we will then speak our truth, see our truth, and hear our truth, at all times. This gives us a wealth of compassion which allows us to be tolerant and kind to others whilst not judging or having an opinion of them or us. This allows us to understand ourselves and others totally, and to be accepting of all situations or circumstances, with the ability to see only good in every situation or person.

When we're our higher/ascended conscious self we maintain our unique power within, all because we have a positive mindset, which allows us to manifest a positive outcome for all. Positive thoughts and actions, go a long way in promoting equilibrium between humankind, nature, and all of creation.

Our ascension is to achieve the ultimate understanding of our truest form and authentic self at all times. We can rebalance to our infinite energy of our ascended self by having commitment, courage, conviction and dedication. Also we need to show compassion, understanding and not to judge us or others, but most of all, to know the true joy of giving to others or us, unconditionally.

There are lots of people in the world today dedicated to ascension, whilst walking the earth plane. Their main objective is to transcend the limitations of our material world, and way of life as we know it. These people would have attained a higher conscious level nearly all of their lives, and our now dedicated to achieving an ascended consciousness whilst walking the earth plane in order to help mankind.

The power within us, is the integration of our collective higher consciousness of all lifetimes. This allows us to embrace the ascended us through initiations and a transformational period that we'll experience for the rest of our lives. We will all eventually return to the ascended master us, within the realms of heaven. Ascended people have not been able to walk the earth plane in many centuries because the vibration of our world would not permit it. With the Age of

Aquarius comes the reawakening of the parts of our brains that have been dormant for centuries. Through the process of initiations, we'll awaken to our ascended us, with us activating incredible powers from within, with the ability to eventually become all knowing.

When you've successfully understood your higher conscious self, and feel empowered by your true inner self and truth, you can balance to your ascended self. This will allow you to feel at one with yourself and the creator. You're thoughts and actions should be of the purest intention, with your vibration making a difference to everyone you meet.

To be enlightened is to be totally dedicated to living your life in truth, by seeing your truth, speaking your truth and hearing your truth at all times. When we our truth we'll be accepting of others version of their truth or even to look at their point of views, allows us to recognise elements of their truth which makes us more accepting, and tolerant of others. With us not being fazed by the choices or decisions that they make, but to be accepting of all situations.

We judge us and others unfairly at times, so we need to offer forgiveness, allowing us to release any grief or guilt that we may have held within. To forgive the self is a hard process, we forgive others far more easily, but to be our power totally we must be able to forgive us. This is important to our continued growth, and allows us to stay healthy of mind, body and soul. We need courage to know ourselves completely, and be proud of who we really are, because this will allow us to recognise our truth at all times, which allows us to become enlightened to the truth of all things.

I have listed below the growth process from the higher conscious self, to the ascended self that allows us to continue our journey of enlightenment.

Levels of Enlightened Growth:

Self Belief: To believe in yourself completely and to reinstate self-belief within.

Self Faith: To have faith in you totally by being realistic in your goals and commitments.

Self Trust: To trust you to make the right decisions, with conviction and courage.

Self Love: To love you and honour and respect you, giving yourself permission to seek the best from life.

Intuition: To listen to your knowing thoughts, truth and not to second guess yourself.

Gut Reaction: To know right from wrong, and to sense when danger maybe lurking.

Knowing Thoughts: To recognise your positive thoughts from our higher/ascended self that requires positive action.

Compassion: To show compassion to you and others and to be compassionate about life.

Non Judgement: Not to judge you or others unfairly, knowing that we are all right in what we do.

Tolerant and Kind: To care for others less fortunate than you, and to encourage and support them.

Acceptance: In acceptance we find the solutions to our problems that save us from pain or grief.

Forgiveness: To forgive ourselves and others, releases us all from blame, knowing we are all right in what we do, and that we can learn and grow together.

Unconditional Love: To love unconditional without a hidden agenda or reward.

Higher consciousness: To recognise your truth and to be your truth, and higher conscious self at all times.

All Knowing: Your knowing thoughts, and to know the difference of your lower conscious thoughts.

Ascension: To see your truth, hear your truth and speak your truth, and to live life with no attachments.

Enlightened: To be enlightened to your truth and life's purpose, and once you've understood and overcome your learning's you can live your life how it was intended.

To be ascended we would only see the good in all things, and oblivious to negativity. We would evolve the limitations of the material world, enjoying a life with no attachments or any preconceived expectations, because everything we need would naturally come to us. We are all individual with different backgrounds, and past life history that's unfolding in order for us to learn from. Our life's lessons and purpose is revealing our truth, and true identities of who we really are, making us whole and complete once more.

Ascension is completion of the soul's quest which then allows us a rebirth, with us seeking love, light and truth in all things. Our ascension path leads us to the understanding of a deeper truth of our existence, and a journey of progress where we achieve more by doing less. When we surrender to the will of creator, his life force energy sustains all growth, and everything we need is within the collective consciousness of humankind.

Stand up straight with your feet apart for balance and connect to the earth, universe and cosmic realms, then also with your mind, body and soul. Place your hand or project your minds energy to your heart centre, and recite the empowered affirmation listed below in a clear decisive manner, then close your eyes, take a deep breath, hold and connect to all things encompassing, allowing your minds energy to expand all the way around you. As you breathe out, say I am my infinite power and allow yourself to rebalance to the power of your ascension whilst in a human form.

The Empowered Affirmation of Ascension:

I now rejoice in my definitive power of ascension, and promise to integrate with all aspects of my truth. I honour and respect the universal laws of conduct, whilst pursuing my continued state of enlightenment whilst residing on the earth plane.

I hope this technique has made a difference to your understanding of what's expected from you, whilst pursing a successful and enjoyable life. I wish you all health, wealth and happiness, in the transition of your higher conscious self embracing the initiation and transformation of your ascended self of uniqueness.

Good luck!

FURTHER INFORMATION

I run numerous Workshops on all aspects of Spiritual & Psychic Awareness, and the Empowered Affirmations Technique.

I am a Life Coach.

A Psychic and Clairvoyant Reader.

I also give Medium-ship.

I am available for Private consultations, group bookings, demonstrations, and seminars.

I also organise Mind, Body, and Spirit Events throughout the U.K, with the aim to go worldwide eventually.

If you need advice on any of the above or if you have any questions, please do not hesitate to email me

veronicalavender@btinternet.com

websites:

www.veronicalavendersholisticevents.co.uk

www.veronicalavender.com

70900402R00065